UNDERSTANDING PEOPLE:

Models and Concepts

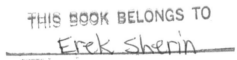

UNDERSTANDING PEOPLE:

Models and Concepts

Walton C. Boshear
Human Relations Consultant
Del Mar, California

Karl G. Albrecht
Human Relations Consultant
San Diego, California

University Associates, Inc.
8517 Production Avenue
P.O. Box 26240
San Diego, California 92126

CONTENTS

FIGURES

INTRODUCTION

This is a book about people. As management consultants, trainers, and facilitators, we find ourselves in the business of helping people to learn about people. The purpose of that learning may be individual growth, improved human relations, increased organization effectiveness, or all of these.

In the course of our work, we have accumulated a "tool kit" of methods and techniques to help us communicate some basic ideas about people and their behavior. Frequently, the tool is no more than a simple diagram and a few words sketched on a flip chart or a chalkboard. Without it, though, we might be limited to groping with abstractions and trading words with little exchange of understanding.

There is a wealth of published material available about human behavior. Any learning facilitator's library is probably well stocked with books and periodicals on philosophy, anthropology, psychology, communications, human behavior, and many other subjects. The presentations of theories and concepts in these books range from the heavily technical to the very superficial. In our association with others in our profession, we have found that facilitators spend much time sifting and sorting through volumes of material to find simple "models" that they can use effectively in the learning environment.

In any learning environment, time is a valuable commodity. Unless a learning program is highly specialized, there is seldom time to explore fully any one theory. The learning facilitator needs methods and techniques for presenting key concepts quickly and to the point. More often than not, his real objective is not to "teach" the theory, but to illuminate a point or process.

Encouraged by friends and associates, we compiled and organized some material that might be useful to the learning facilitator. To test the project, we organized a seminar that attracted trainers, facilitators, consultants, and others in the learning and helping professions.

The post-seminar evaluations showed that this material was valuable and useful to these people in their work. But to our surprise, most of the participants' comments focused on their *personal* learning. Apparently, exposure to a broad range of models had facilitated feelings of personal growth, awareness, and confidence in these individuals—apart from the value of the models to them as training tools.

The seminar experience prompted us to try out the program on people who were not in the learning professions. We set up classes at adult schools and community colleges, and we conducted seminars in the business environment. The enthusiastic reception given to these programs was our final confirmation. These models were valuable, not only as *training* aids, but also as *learning* aids.

What Is a Model?

So far, we have been using the term *model* rather freely. We would like to offer a fairly specific working definition and to share the process by which it was derived.

Very early in compiling our materials we confronted the question "What *is* a model?" Initially, a specific answer to the question was very elusive. We were aware of some typical scientific definitions such as *a model is a symbolic representation of the functions or aspects of a system or a complex event and their interrelationships*. But none of the scientific or technical definitions seemed really to capture our ideas about the models we were working with. Labeling some tools as models and others as merely useful concepts, we could not always make a clear distinction between the two.

Somewhat subjectively, we began sorting the vast amount of material into models and "not-models." As we worked on the models, shaping them into a consistent format and treatment, a definition emerged. What we had done, it seems, is suggested by the following story:

> The teacher observed that Jimmy, in the back row, was deeply intent on some work at his desk. Nose-to-paper, fingers gripping his pencil tightly, he was engrossed in drawing a picture.
> "What are you drawing, Jimmy?" inquired the teacher.
> Without looking up, Jimmy replied, "I'm drawing a picture of God."
> Taken aback, the teacher responded, "But Jimmy, no one really knows what God looks like."
> "That's OK," Jimmy observed. "They will when I get this picture finished."

Although we did not know exactly what a model was, we continued to "draw the picture" anyway. While developing a classification system, we were able to describe the criteria we had been unconsciously applying. We arrived at an *operational* definition of a model as a conceptual framework that:

- Has a definite scope, encompassing a particular body of information from the real world;
- Defines the data elements within its scope of application;
- Structures the information in a way that can be diagrammed;
- Describes relationships between the data elements; and
- Permits inferences that can be demonstrated by real-world experiences.

Many models used in everyday life become so familiar that they are not recognized as models. People use calendars, vacation schedules, checkbooks, and computer logic diagrams without thinking about them as models. Through long use, they have come intuitively to understand the scope, definitions, and data relationships of these models. Individuals use the models simply to record the structure of the data, consulting them from time to time both to refresh their memory of the structure and to draw inferences that can be used in conducting daily business.

One important characteristic of the modeling process makes it very valuable. Take the checkbook as an example. An exceptional person, with high powers of concentration and the ability to retain figures in his head, might be able to keep track of his bank deposits and withdrawals. He might be able to know or predict when he is overdrawn. But with the checkbook as a model of the account status, the same knowledge is available to an individual of ordinary ability. Through the modeling process, each step of which is quite simple, he can get an overall picture of the results of individual transactions. It is the merging of data, definitions, structure, and their relationships that brings this new knowledge.

Criteria for Inclusion

Within our definition of a model, we established some criteria for inclusion. In our opinion, the models selected for this book meet the following criteria:

Scope. The model covers a body of information that is relevant to learning about people, and it deals with subjects that are likely to be encountered in the typical learning situation.

Definitions. Definitions of the data elements are straightforward and avoid the use of obscure terminology or concepts. We favor models that use everyday words to discuss basic ideas and their implications.

Structure. The model provides a simple, but very useful, organization of data, and it can be quickly and easily diagrammed. Complex diagrams and structures are avoided, not because they might not be valuable in their implications, but because they are not consistent with our intent.

Relationships. Relationships between the data elements in the model are obvious or easily demonstrated. We favor those that make sense without resorting to elaborate or complicated reasoning processes.

Inferences. At least a few useful first-order inferences can be drawn from the model and demonstrated within the learning situation. A demonstration might include calling upon the experiences of the participants, observing an ongoing process, or conducting a simple experiment or exercise.

Origins of Models

Some of the models and concepts included here originated with us. More often, however, the models came from work done by others. Many of these were taken almost intact from their sources.

For clarity, we modified some models. Wherever possible, we replaced technical terminology with a word or a phrase used in everyday conversation. Many of the changes were minor, others were the result of condensing entire volumes into a brief model. In every case, we tried to provide the source of the model. We wanted to give credit to the model's originator and to guide the reader to a more comprehensive treatment of the material.

Holding the book to a convenient length prevented the inclusion of supporting data to validate models. Consequently, we offer this material with only one claim—it has been useful to us. If any model or concept does not seem to make sense, the reader should either abandon it or dig into the reference material for more information. For us, the most successful models are those that "click" right away.

Organization of Material

Each model is offered as a self-contained learning module, usable as it is without reference to other materials, either inside or outside the book. We have attempted to present the model objectively in terms of the five key criteria categories: scope, definitions, structure, relationships, and inferences. However, we have not labeled these five elements because their order changes from model to model, according to the need for logical development and clear communication of ideas.

Following the presentation of each model is a discussion of some ideas we have about the model. This discussion includes suggestions, and some cautions, about the use of the model. In many cases the suggestions developed from our own experience in demonstrating the model in the learning situation. Wherever possible, each presentation ends with some principal references to a more comprehensive treatment of the subject.

The individual models are loosely gathered together under five topic headings: Individuals, Dyads, Groups, Organizations, and Problem Solving. Rather than develop a rigorous classification system within the major categories, we arranged the models in what seems to be a logical sequence, providing a natural flow for reading.

Obviously, all the models in the field could not be treated in depth; our selection is a basic inventory. Other concepts that may prove useful are described briefly in Part Six, each with a single reference (when available) to a principal resource.

A final part, Applications of the Models, contains some of our experiences and thoughts on the subject of models in general. There we explore some of the general characteristics of models, the development and application of models, and some comparisons between them.

PART 1
INDIVIDUAL MODELS

INTRODUCTION TO
INDIVIDUAL MODELS

Since the late nineteenth century, an ever-increasing number of theories have been advanced to describe "the way people are." From Freud's beginnings sprang a veritable family tree of therapeutic models. Parallel to the growth of Freudian ideas, and perhaps as a result of the general activity level, entirely new concepts have developed. Many of these have evolved from psychotherapy and psychoanalysis. However, insofar as psychiatric models describe a selected range of so-called abnormal behavior, they sometimes do not account for much of what is normal and important about people.

More recently, another movement has taken shape, roughly termed humanistic psychology. Oriented toward individual growth, humanistic psychology focuses on understanding oneself, rather than on passive submission to treatment. As a field of experimentation, observation, and conjecture, humanistic psychology has produced a number of very useful models for describing the feelings and behavior of people. These models deal primarily with the so-called normal human activities and processes that are part of the business of living.

In behavioral science, as in other branches of science, ideas do not usually occur first in their simplest form. Individual discoveries are collected, combined, sifted, and "massaged" until an underlying structure emerges. As ideas are combined in different ways, divergent schools of thought are derived, such as Freudians, Adlerians, Jungians, Existentialists, Gestaltists, Behaviorists, Humanists, etc. The individual-oriented models in this first section range across a wide spectrum and, in many cases, can be traced to classical points of view. They provide convenient ways of thinking and communicating about people in terms of their motivations, thoughts, feelings, and behavior.

1 Assumptions About Human Nature

Behind much of an individual's behavior and relations with other people are the basic assumptions he makes about the "nature of man." The Assumptions About Human Nature Model identifies three common sets of assumptions that lead to significant variations in strategies for behaving with others. This particular version of the model is an adaptation of the work of several people who have developed similar models for individual or organizational applications.

Many people hold one of three alternative views or "theories" about human nature: *animalistic, humanistic,* or *rational.* This model does not contend that human beings actually do fall into one of these categories, but that people frequently behave as though *others,* in fact, fit neatly under one of these labels.

Animalistic. According to the animalistic viewpoint, the nature of the human being is no different from that of other animals. Driven by biological urges and seeking gratification of those urges, human animals must be controlled by laws, mores, and other civilizing structures of society.

Humanistic. From the humanistic perspective, a person is driven by humane considerations for self and others—kindness, mercy, and compassion. The humanistic individual is self-actualizing—seeking the realization of his own inherent potential. There is little need for external control, since an individual will exercise self-control through concern for others.

Rational. The third "theory" assumes people are rational beings; they are inherently neither good nor evil. Driven by his intellect and seeking to find reason in all things, the individual is controlled by logical thinking and by evaluation of the consequence of his actions for himself and others.

Each of the three alternative sets of assumptions about the nature of man is categorized, along with associated characteristics, in Figure 1.

Implications of the Model

Figure 1 shows that by accepting any characteristics listed in a particular row—*Drives, Goals, Nature,* or *Controls*—one also accepts the basic assumption about people implied by the column heading. The assumptions

	ANIMALISTIC	HUMANISTIC	RATIONAL
DRIVES	Physical	Humanism	Intellect
GOALS	Gratification	Self-Actualizing	Reason
NATURE	Evil	Good	Neither
CONTROLS	Civilization	Compassion	Logic

Figure 1. Three assumptions about human nature

we make about ourselves and others will determine the way we approach other people and the way we establish and maintain relationships with them.

If we embrace the animalistic theory, we will probably approach others warily and competitively. We will feel a need to protect ourselves. We will not "let down our guard" around other people or trust them with information that might be used to harm us. We search for ways to establish and maintain controls over their behavior.

Our approach to other people will be very different if we see them as humanistic. Because we assume that they will not hurt us intentionally, we will trust them. We will be cooperative. The only controls needed in the humanistic view are informational: let people know that something they are doing is harmful, and they will attempt to modify their behavior.

If we see people as rational beings, we may negotiate with them on a logical basis for mutually beneficial and compatible behaviors. We may share with them our feelings, attitudes, needs, and goals, and work with them toward equitable and reasonable solutions to problems.

DISCUSSION

This model is useful in setting the stage for people to explore their feelings about themselves and others. They may contrast the process of generalizing about people with the process of making individual or situational decisions. They may examine racial or social stereotypes and some of the assumptions that nurture them.

Frequently people hold different assumptions about themselves than they do about other people. This model provides a focus for examining and discussing the reasons why an individual places himself in one category and everyone else in another.

Sometimes using this model encourages the externalizing of its concepts. This may be quite acceptable in the academic environment and may even be the reason for introducing the model. But in the experiential situation, it may lead individuals away from the here-and-now, and toward abstracting their feelings. To avoid this tendency, the presentation of the model should be closely followed with a structured experience or some other exercise that encourages participants to explore and share the implications of the model.

There is another discomforting tendency of this model. It strongly suggests an either/or choice of the assumption. It does not clearly allow for intermediate positions, nor does it suggest differing intensities of the orientations. These aspects, if relevant, must be dealt with separately.

SUGGESTED READINGS

Hall, C. S. *A primer of Freudian psychology.* New York: Mentor Books, 1954.

Jones, J. E. Assumptions about the nature of man. In J. W. Pfeiffer & J. E. Jones (Eds.), *The 1972 annual handbook for group facilitators.* La Jolla, Calif.: University Associates, 1972.

Maslow, A. H. *Toward a psychology of being* (2nd ed.). New York: Van Nostrand Reinhold, 1968.

McGregor, D. *The human side of enterprise.* New York: McGraw-Hill, 1961.

Reddin, W. J., & Sullivan, J. B. XYZ test. In J. W. Pfeiffer & R. Heslin, *Instrumentation in human relations training.* La Jolla, Calif.: University Associates, 1973.

Robinson, A. J. McGregor's theory X—theory Y model. In J. W. Pfeiffer & J. E. Jones (Eds.), *The 1972 annual handbook for group facilitators.* La Jolla, Calif.: University Associates, 1972.

2 Ego States: Parent Adult Child

The Parent/Adult/Child Model, developed by Eric Berne, explains and classifies individual behavior as originating in one of three possible *ego states*: the Parent, the Adult, or the Child. (Within the model, these common terms are given specialized definitions, which are explained later.) An ego state may be regarded as a consistent arrangement of thoughts and feelings. In response to his immediate experience, an individual adopts one of the three basic ego states, and his behavior takes on a pattern that is characteristic of that ego state. A study of ego states forms the basis for Berne's transactional analysis, which is a theory of personality and group dynamics and also a therapeutic method. The following are brief descriptions of the three ego states.[1]

Adult. The Adult ego state is characterized by rational thought, information processing, reality testing, comparing, and decision making. Emotion is not considered to be a component of the Adult state. In the context of this model, the term Adult does not imply any particular connotation such as "maturity." It simply describes the unemotional state in which rational thought processes are carried out.

Child. The Child ego state is the configuration dominated by emotions. An individual is said to be in the Child state when he is experiencing and expressing—or is just experiencing—any of the feelings that we commonly associate with childhood: joy, gaiety, jubilation, delight, anger, rage, hostility, etc. The term Child does not imply immaturity. Its meaning is closer to *childlike* than to *childish*.

Parent. The third ego state, the Parent, is the source of values, judgments, prohibitions, and injunctions—all of the *shoulds* and *should nots*—the guidelines and standards for living. It contains the accumulated record of social programming, cultural traditions, and responsibilities. The internal Parent draws judgments largely from information received from the individual's natural parents and from other significant parent-like figures who populate his early life.

---

1. Ego states are also described in Models 11 and 18.

Figure 2 represents the individual in terms of the three ego states. The structural arrangement of the diagram demonstrates the role of the Adult, "between" the Parent and the Child, to integrate the influence of each and to make appropriate responses to the environment.

Individual Development

In association with the P/A/C Model, Berne proposed a theory of individual development to explain the formulation of the three ego states and the relationships among them.

The *little person* (the term child has been mortgaged in this case to a specialized vocabulary) enters the world driven primarily by physical needs: air, water, food, elimination, warmth, and affection. When these needs are met, and he is physically comfortable, he feels good and secure. When they are not met, he feels pain and discomfort. These feelings are permanently "recorded" in each little person's brain as he grows. This collection of "tapes" becomes the Child ego state.

As the little person grows, he receives many signals about the way he should and should not act. Certain behavior is not based on a logical interaction with his environment but is simply given to him by significant guides in his early life, usually his mother and father. His Parent state becomes a collection of these guidance data. Parent data are largely *imitative*, especially until the little person's Adult is sufficiently developed.

The Adult state results from the little person's attempts to reason about his world. He begins learning how to make choices, to visualize people and objects beyond his immediate perception, and to take these into account in his actions. The Adult ego state stores logical data about the operation of the world.

The role of the Adult in evaluating the environment and in regulating the ego state from which he responds presumes some form of free will. However, in order for this condition to prevail, the individual must establish and maintain a flexibility that allows responses appropriate to real-life circumstances and brings desired results. If the person's Adult ego state is *contaminated* by one or both of the other ego states, he will be limited to a truncated set of behavioral options in transactions with others.

Parent and Child Functions

It is useful to consider two aspects for each of the Parent and Child states and to clarify their functions. These labels for the Parent functions describe their impact on the internal Child and their influence on the individual's relationships with others:

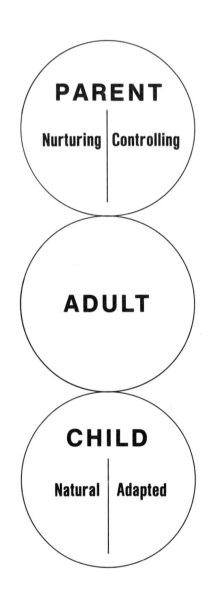

Figure 2. Structural diagram of Parent/Adult/Child ego states (Adapted from Berne 1964)

1. *The Controlling Parent* sets limits, disciplines, judges, and criticizes feelings and behavior.

2. *The Nurturing Parent* guides, protects, teaches, and gives advice.

Subdivisions of the Child ego state also have self-explanatory titles:

1. *The Natural Child* implies an uninhibited, free-wheeling expression of emotions and feelings that may be loving, spontaneous, creative, fun-loving, exciting, adventurous, trusting, and joyful.

2. *The Adapted Child*, on the other hand, refers to the state of suppressed emotions that results from the internal Parent's continued influence on the Child. The behaviors of the Adapted Child are likely to range through anger, rebellion, fear and conformity.

The P/A/C Model offers a very reactive concept of personality development. It suggests that, unless significant personality changes take place, the grownup person is highly programmed. He carries with him a collection of emotional reaction patterns, beliefs, values, responsibilities, and a sense of propriety that he has derived from a small handful of people.

DISCUSSION

The P/A/C Model is a remarkably comprehensive tool for clarifying basic features of behavior and for exploring personal relationships. Though simple in construction, its implications are vast. An entire system of group therapy, transactional analysis, has been developed around its basic concepts. Much of the usefulness of the model stems from the simplicity of its definitions and structure and the range of inferences that can be drawn from them.

The following are just a few of the subjects that can be introduced and explored in a learning group with the aid of the P/A/C Model:

Prejudice: the excessive influence or contamination of the Adult by the Parent;

Free will to change: the capacity of the Adult to adapt the ego state to the situation;

Guilt: the internal function of the Parent in punishing the Child for certain types of feelings or behavior;

Self-image: the Child state as the source of basic attitudes about oneself;

Two-person transactions: managing the ego states of oneself and the other person in order to carry out a successful problem-solving transaction, e.g., supervisor and employee.

If it is presented early in a learning situation concerned with individual behavior, the P/A/C Model provides a fundamental framework useful for later reference and clarification of more complex concepts.

A minor drawback of the model is the set of special definitions that are given to the words Parent, Adult, and Child. These words are so commonly used and have such powerful connotations for most people— either positive or negative—that a special effort must be made to communicate the definitions offered by the model in such a way that they will be discriminated from the existing definitions.

The model may be introduced and frequently recalled in order to focus on group processes. The model provides a vocabulary with which the group members can communicate about certain types of patterned behaviors within the group. Not only is it a relatively nonthreatening way to examine those behaviors, but it provides some specific alternatives with which group members can experiment. They may use the concepts of Parent, Adult, and Child as roles for exploring consequences of different types of behavior.

SUGGESTED READINGS

Anderson, J. P. A transactional analysis primer. In J. E. Jones & J. W. Pfeiffer (Eds.), *The 1973 annual handbook for group facilitators.* La Jolla, Calif.: University Associates, 1973.

Berne, E. *Transactional analysis in psychotherapy.* New York: Grove Press, 1961.

Berne, E. *Games people play.* New York: Grove Press, 1964.

Berne, E. *What do you say after you say hello?* New York: Grove Press, 1972.

3 OK—NOT OK Life Positions

The Life Positions Model is an integral part of Eric Berne's work in transactional analysis. It was explored by Thomas Harris as a separate model for understanding individual behavior. The model provides a conceptual framework for understanding an individual in terms of whether he sees himself and others as either OK or NOT OK. OK feelings are characterized by a sense of power, capability, well-being, lovableness, and personal worth. NOT OK feelings are the opposite: weakness, inability, helplessness, insignificance, anxiety, being unlovable, and lack of personal worth.

Four Extreme Positions

The Life Positions Model is based on the idea that each individual adopts an attitude of being *generally* OK or *generally* NOT OK and also attributes either an OK or NOT OK status to those around him. Early in childhood, most people develop a basic life position with respect to being OK which is rarely abandoned and, in fact, is usually reinforced by the individual's selective perceptions and reactions to his experiences. The model describes four extreme life positions associated with possible combinations of OK-ness or NOT OK-ness as seen in oneself and attributed to others. The combinations are the following.

I'm NOT OK—You're OK. In this position, a person tends to accept a psychologically inferior orientation to others in situations that concern his competence, influence, or personal power. Burdened with self-defeating attitudes and lack of confidence, a person in this position believes he cannot measure up to other people.

I'm NOT OK—You're NOT OK. This position implies a highly maladjusted personality: An individual believes that he is worthless—and so is everyone else. Suspicious of others, he becomes anxious about what he or others might do that will be harmful to him. Such a person feels disconnected from other people and alienated from his environment. But he has little motivation to try to do anything about his feeling.

I'm OK—*You're* NOT OK. In this position, a person believes he cannot rely on anyone but himself. He feels that people around him are worthless or may be enemies, and his life will be fine if people will just leave him alone. No matter what happens it is always someone else's fault. Because the individual in this life position cannot depend upon anyone but himself, he soon learns to provide his own internal satisfactions.

I'm OK—*You're* OK. In the fourth life position, the person sees himself as interdependent with others and with his environment. Although he accepts and appreciates signals from others confirming his OK-ness, he does not depend upon them. Because this individual has accepted the responsibility for his own OK-ness, he has no difficulty in attributing OK-ness to others.

Berne postulates that the first three life positions are consequences of particular experiences in childhood. However, the fourth position represents a perceptual jump from the other positions. It can only be reached by a conscious re-evaluation of one's self-concept. Figure 3 represents the structural relationships of the four basic life positions. The area within the square represents all possible life positions, with the four extreme positions represented at the corners. The dotted line suggests the perceptual jump required to achieve the fourth life position.

Development of Life Positions

Analyzing the development of the basic life positions can lead toward understanding their nature and consequences. In his early life, the infant has a mixture of OK and NOT OK feelings, with the NOT OK feelings predominating. The infant can feel OK when his physical needs are satisfied and when he receives positive *strokes* (physical attention, recognition, and affection) from those who care for him. When his needs are not met, he feels NOT OK. Simply because he is small, powerless, and inept, the little person's early experiences provide him with a large share of negative strokes. Withheld or negative stroking is not necessarily deliberate, but may result from the little person's inability to communicate his needs. Because big people have the capacity to satisfy his needs or not, as they see fit, he views them as all-powerful. Without question, the little person assumes that they are all OK. In fact, since they are the source of his well being, it would be terrifying for him to believe otherwise.

For most people, the early I'm NOT OK—You're OK position becomes a habit of life they continue into adulthood. Nothing of enough psychological magnitude ever happens to cause them to re-evaluate this position.

A preponderance of negative or withheld strokes may force the little

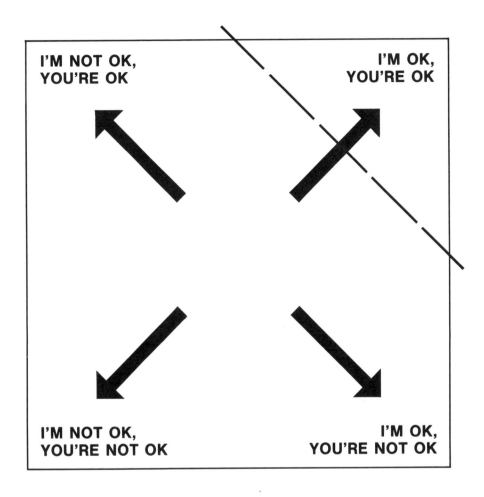

I'M NOT OK,
YOU'RE OK

I'M OK,
YOU'RE OK

I'M NOT OK,
YOU'RE NOT OK

I'M OK,
YOU'RE NOT OK

Figure 3. **Structural diagram of the basic life positions**
(Adapted from Harris 1967)

person to withdraw—he may switch to one of the other basic life positions. The battered child who receives much pain from the big people around him may eventually be forced to conclude that they are NOT OK. He re-evaluates his situation after being overwhelmed by physical abuse. If his internal resources are such that he can satisfy his own needs for stroking, the little person concludes that he is OK, and it is only the big people who are NOT OK. He would be fine if it were not for them.

If the little person's early experiences with negative or withheld strokes are not powerful enough to make him re-evaluate his basic position—perhaps affection is withheld or he is neglected—he may merely revise his opinion of others. He still feels his own NOT OK-ness, but now he extends that to others as well.

In the absence of some powerful stimulus or motivation, whichever of these three basic life positions the little person assumes will remain unaltered throughout his life and will influence him in all his interactions with others.

DISCUSSION

The Life Positions Model is useful in almost any learning situation related to people and their behavior. The focus can be on the ways in which the different life positions are developed and fixed in the individual, or attention can be directed to the consequences of the individual's life positions.

The usefulness of this model is enhanced by its simple vocabulary and by the fact that relevant examples of the basic life positions can be elicited from almost any group.

One of the minor disadvantages of the model springs from its popularity. At a surface level, it is widely known, which is not to say that it is widely understood. The terms OK and NOT OK have become conversational patter for many people, and that dilutes the model's impact. This disadvantage can be overcome by encouraging group members to examine their own here-and-now experiences and discover their own positions.

In the experiential learning situation, the Life Positions Model can make a strong impact at the point when individuals within the group are wrestling with their own self-concepts. When they have become intuitively aware of, and dissatisfied with, the NOT OK life position, the model can introduce some positive direction for continued growth. This is particularly true if an individual's option to choose the fourth position is emphasized. Although it will have less impact, the model may be used for setting goals early in the development of the group.

SUGGESTED READINGS

Berne, E. *Transactional analysis in psychotherapy.* New York: Grove Press, 1961.

Berne, E. *What do you say after you say hello?* New York: Grove Press, 1972.

Harris, T. A. *I'm OK—You're OK: A practical guide to transactional analysis.* New York: Harper & Row, 1967.

Meininger, J. *Success through transactional analysis.* New York: New American Library, 1973.

4 Hierarchy of Human Needs

The Hierarchy of Human Needs Model, developed by Abraham Maslow, classifies *needs*, the internal drives for satisfaction that give rise to human behavior. An unsatisfied need creates tension, either unpleasant or pleasant; it energizes and motivates the individual's behavior.

According to Maslow, when a person behaves in such a way that one need is satisfied, then other needs begin to manifest themselves. There are always needs demanding satisfaction. Certain needs, however, take priority over others. A high-priority need will dominate behavior until it is satisfied, at least partially. Then it will give way to other needs with lower priorities.

Human needs are classified by the model into the following five categories, according to their priorities for satisfaction.

Basic (survival) needs: air, water, food, shelter;

Safety needs: to know that one's survival is not in jeopardy;

Belongingness (social) needs: to be accepted by others; to be a part of one's social environment;

Ego-Status needs: to feel significant, effectual, and competent; to have self-esteem;

Self-Actualization needs: to grow and expand one's personal horizons; to become all that one can become; to challenge oneself.

Figure 4 shows the hierarchy of needs as five levels of a pyramid. This representation of the model is commonly used to portray the priority nature of the needs.

Satisfying Needs

Clearly, the physiological needs at *Level One (Basic Survival)* will dominate behavior if they are not satisfied. If a person cannot breathe, or is very hungry or thirsty, no other need will be significant enough to domnate his behavior. And the person who is physically comfortable will try to insure the continuation of that condition.

24

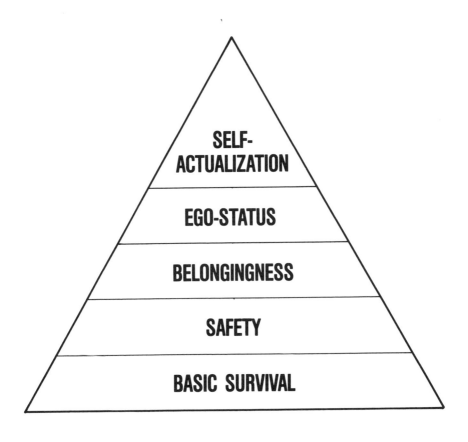

Figure 4. Maslow's hierarchy of human needs
(Data for diagram based on Hierarchy of Needs in "A Theory of Human Motiva-
tion" in *Motivation and Personality*, 2nd Edition by Abraham H. Maslow. Harper &
Row, 1970.)

Level Two (Safety) needs are often met in more indirect ways, such as an adequate salary, insurance, or a burglar alarm system to reduce tension.

Level Three (Belongingness) needs are satisfied through social behavior—friendship, group membership, and family ties. Once comfortable and secure, a person will turn his attention to his relationships with others. To satisfy the need to be accepted and appreciated by his social peer groups, a person must learn a minimum inventory of social skills.

Level Four (Ego-Status) needs demand considerably more sophistication from the individual if they are to be satisfied. At this ego satisfaction level, a person is heavily dependent upon the responses of others for needs satisfaction. He must learn to manage his transactions with others, often over an extended period of time, in order to achieve the satisfaction of needs at this level.

Level Five (Self-Actualization) is a highly abstract need category and accounts for the wide variety of human behavior aimed at self-expression. Many aspects of our culture—painting, sculpture, music, architecture, literature—seem to arise from a human compulsion to manifest thoughts and feelings. In addition, simply challenging oneself can often satisfy self-actualizing needs. The need for self-actualization seems to be the basis for human creativity.

The Needs Hierarchy Model implies that human behavior is highly ordered, arising from patterns that are rather consistent across our culture. Behavior is also a priority system of actions, serving always to reduce the tension with which needs manifest themselves.

One of the important implications of the model is that human behavior can be predicted to some extent. That is, if we know something about the current needs of an individual, we can forecast, in general terms, the patterns of his behavior.

DISCUSSION

The Needs Hierarchy Model focuses attention on the causes of human behavior, and one of the most fruitful areas of application is in management and supervision. In these situations, the model can help to identify misconceptions about motivating employees. The supervisor or manager may well be trying to appeal to levels of needs—basic survival and safety—which no longer exert significant pressure on the individual. Although most people in today's society would like to have more pay for their work, other needs may actually take priority in influencing their behavior.

In using the Needs Hierarchy Model, it is important to recognize some of the conceptual limitations of the model structure. The model, as presented, does not account for the *intensity* of the various need pressures. For example, the model would not readily predict such idealistic behavior as starving for one's art, committing ritual suicide, going to jail as a form of social protest, and taking extreme risks in athletics or physical adventure. Although not necessarily excluded from the scope of the hierarchy-of-needs theory, these forms of behavior are not readily inferred from the model structure and definitions.

The symbolism of space and geometry which we in the Western culture carry around with us play a strong role in this model. Placing basic needs at the bottom and self-actualization at the top, while necessary to the hierarchy concept, subtly suggests that some needs are better than others. These spatial implications must be countered when applying the hierarchy model.

Another questionable implication of the model structure is the apparent isolation of the need categories from each other, even though the categories are not necessarily discrete in terms of behavior. For example, seeking social approval of one's actions might serve, under certain circumstances, to satisfy needs in several of the categories.

We offer one more caution. A user of the model might be tempted to try to adapt it to a quantitative end—by applying some sort of measurement scale. For example, one might wish to picture an individual as residing momentarily at some altitude on a vertical scale. This would be an extension of the model beyond the realm of its intention.

SUGGESTED READINGS

Maslow, A. H. A theory of human motivation. *Psychological Review*, 1943, 50, 370-396.

Maslow, A. H. *Toward a psychology of being* (2nd ed.). New York: Van Nostrand Reinhold, 1968.

Maslow, A. H. *Motivation and personality* (2nd ed.). New York: Harper & Row, 1970.

Pfeiffer, S. L. The Maslow need hierarchy. In J. W. Pfeiffer & J. E. Jones (Eds.), *The 1972 annual handbook for group facilitators*. La Jolla, Calif.: University Associates, 1972.

5 Cognitive Dissonance

The Cognitive Dissonance Model concerns the *dissonance* created within the human brain when a conflict exists between two ideas accepted by the individual as true. Leon Festinger, who developed the model, postulated that the presence of this dissonance motivates the individual to eliminate or reduce it in order to achieve consistency.

Cognitive Elements

Thoughts, ideas, beliefs, values, and known facts are categorized by the model as the basic *cognitive elements*. A *cognitive cluster*, a collection of elements forming a self-consistent unit, is also referred to as a cognitive element.

Any two cognitive elements are characterized as either *irrelevant* to each other, or *relevent*. Pairs of elements that are irrelevant, such as "I like George" and "two plus two equals four," do not produce dissonance. Because the individual perceives no particular connection between the two concepts or ideas, there can be no conflict for him.

Elements that are relevant to each other can be either *consonant* (in agreement), or *dissonant* (in conflict). If they are consonant—"I like George" and "I must work with George"—no conflict arises and, therefore, they do not modify the individual's behavior. It is the area of *dissonance* between *relevant* cognitive elements—"I dislike George" and "I must work with George"—that is the subject of this model. The behavioral influences of cognitive elements are summarized in Figure 5.

The Cognitive Dissonance Model describes conventional, normal cognitive processes common to all human beings. Festinger did not see cognitive dissonance as a pathological condition, but as a consequence of the ways in which the brain accumulates and interrelates information.

The scope of the model extends to the relative importance of the cognitive elements to the individual. This leads to the notion of *magnitude* of dissonance. Dissonance produced by the relationship of two elements which are both important to the individual can be expected to influence behavior more extensively than would the dissonance between two elements of no particular significance. An intermediate level of dissonance

28

Relationship between cognitive elements	Compatibility of cognitive elements	Influence on behavior
Irrelevant	Neither consonant nor dissonant	None
Relevant	Consonant	None
	Dissonant	Pressure to reduce dissonance

Figure 5. Behavioral influence of cognitive elements

29

would arise between a cognitive element of great importance and one of little importance.

The Cognitive Dissonance Model has direct application to the decision-making process. None of the choices in a decision-making situation are likely to be entirely desirable or completely undesirable. In most cases, no matter which choice is made, some desirable aspects will be rejected and some undesirable aspects will be acquired. At the moment of decision, dissonance arises as a consequence of the conflict between the knowledge of the action taken ("I got a good buy on a car,") and the undesirable aspects of the action ("I'm having trouble with it"). At the same time, dissonance arises from the conflict between the knowledge of the action taken ("I bought a new car") and the desirable aspect of the unchosen alternative ("I liked the looks of my old car").

Reduction of Dissonance

In his research, Festinger discovered that people behave in many different ways to reduce dissonance. Principally, they may:

- manipulate the environment to change one or more of the facts;
- gather information to support or discount one or more of the cognitive elements; and
- decrease the relative importance of both of the elements.

The first of these methods is a direct response. The latter two, however, have important implications in the area of *input selection*. The Cognitive Dissonance Model implies that an individual will pay attention to information that will avoid, reduce, or eliminate dissonance. Information that creates or increases dissonance will be filtered or distorted by perceptual mechanisms. In the absence of external sources of information, the individual will engage in *conceptual* manipulation to create patterns and relationships that result in minimum dissonance between cognitive elements.

DISCUSSION

The Cognitive Dissonance Model is conceptually simple, but its applications are not necessarily so. Working with it in teaching and consulting situations can increase understanding of the model and its potential. It is worthy of careful attention and reflection by anyone concerned with people and with the cognitive processes of decision making, life planning, or attitude reprogramming.

In the traditional lecture-discussion situation, the model is a useful discussion tool for drawing the attention of the group to the realities of human cognitive processes. Innumerable examples from real life can be coupled with the model to demonstrate its concepts. It encourages group participants to broaden their views of so-called objective thinking and of problem solving.

The model offers some useful concepts for dealing with human growth and change processes. If we view personal growth as a learning process, then the individual's strategies for avoiding or reducing dissonance may inhibit his acceptance of any information that could facilitate beneficial change. Consider, for example, the person whose childhood environment firmly impresses upon him the belief that he is stupid. According to the Cognitive Dissonance Model, he will selectively collect information that is relevant and consonant with this belief. If new information disagrees with his self-concept, the individual is likely to distort or misunderstand it in order to avoid dissonance.

It is possible to design growth-oriented learning environments that introduce new information, and also reduce dissonance, thus facilitating assimilation of the new information. This can result in a change of self-concept. In this regard, the model aids in the design of experiential learning situations.

The model has been especially useful in learning situations where decision making plays a key role, such as management and supervisory development. Because business life is rich with large and small decisions, many examples are always at hand. The discussion from the model can be led in two directions: (1) analyzing various types of decisions and why they produce dissonance; and (2) examining the ways in which people attempt to reduce post-decision dissonance.

A limitation of the model is its narrow scope; it covers primarily cognitive processes. It does not examine the broad spectrum of feelings and their resultant behavioral implications. Perhaps because of this, the model has only limited applications in the experiential learning situation. On occasion, it has provided some insight into the anxious feelings experienced by group members after they have made a decision of some magnitude or when they have just reached a significant turning point in the group's life. Discussing the model, group members may explore the sources of the dissonance and share these concerns and feelings with each other as a means of reducing the dissonance.

SUGGESTED READING

Festinger, L. *A theory of cognitive dissonance.* Stanford, Calif.: Stanford University Press, 1957.

The Structural Differential

The Structural Differential Model deals with the basic psychological processes underlying verbal thought and communication. Alfred Korzybski developed the model to illustrate limitations and potential pitfalls inherent in the use of words. The Structural Differential Model occupies a central position in Korzybski's comprehensive theory of general semantics, a theory that others who came after him have extended and popularized.

At the foundation of the model is the concept of an *objective world* that has a natural structure. From the microscopic to the macroscopic, the objective world is viewed as a dynamic and ever-changing *process* within certain patterns of natural structure. Similarly, language, which serves as the basis for thought and communication, also has a structure. It is within the rules and constraints of language structure that concepts and ideas are created and manipulated. Korzybski maintained that the *differential* between these two structures represents the source of many of the difficulties an individual has in dealing effectively with his environment.

The Structural Differential Model specifically examines the process by which a person makes the *transition* from the structure of the objective world to his interior world of words and abstract concepts. This transitional process is diagrammatically represented in Figure 6. The Structural Differential Model can perhaps be best understood by following the process step by step.

Perceptual Abstraction. Of the unlimited number of events that take place in the world around the individual, his senses permit him to acquire only a tiny sample. The diagram suggests that as a person pays attention to certain perceivable processes, he necessarily leaves out all else. Korzybski referred to this sensory selection process as *abstracting*. This initial, preverbal perception is the *first-order* abstraction.

Perceptual-Verbal Transition. Following the first-order abstraction, the individual makes a gigantic leap, or transition, to the *verbal level*, where he applies labels to his perceptual abstractions. These labels, or *descriptions*, are *second-order abstractions*. It is at this point that the individual leaves the structure of the objective world and enters the structure of language.

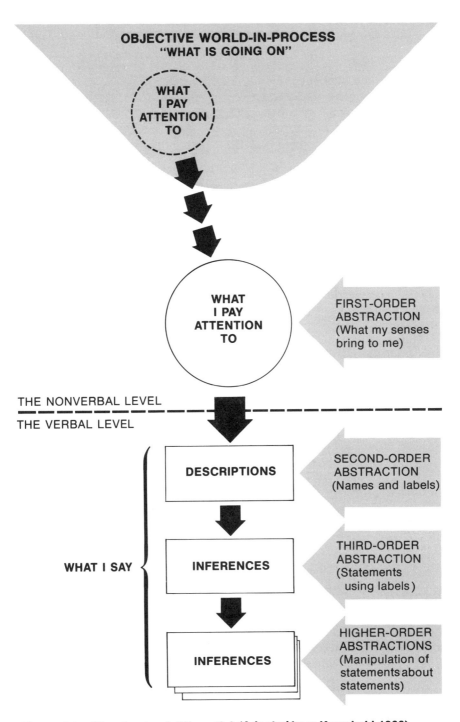

Figure 6.1.   The structural differential (Adapted from Korsybski 1933)

33

Verbal Abstraction. The next level of the model represents third-order abstraction. Because the previous level consisted of labels, the individual now makes *statements using labels*. At this level, he assembles verbal symbols to create new patterns of thought. These patterns are not necessarily represented in the process world; they are *inferences*, statements about the world not derived from direct perceptual abstraction.

As the diagram indicates, the individual can continue to move through higher-order abstractions, making statements about statements. Presumably, there is no limit to this process of making inferences from inferences.

The model represents all statements as abstractions of one level or another, and it implies the existence of a "ladder" of abstraction. A simple example of this feature of language is the sequence of abstractions leading from a nonverbal *object of perception* to the descriptive name "Fido," to the level of "Irish terrier," to "dog," to "canine," to "animal," etc. Some of these abstractions are very far removed from the process world of direct perception.

This model states that the verbal world has a structure of its own, separate from the structure of the process world. Inasmuch as any language imposes rules upon the brain's manipulation of words, it follows that structural flaws in the language will lead to flaws in thinking and communicating about the objective world. Korzybski noted the following key structural flaws in English.

> *Static view of reality*. Extensive use of the labeling function of language, supported by the overused word *is*, leads a person to think of the world as a static, unchanging place, and to think of himself as a static, unchanging creature.
>
> *Elementalistic descriptions*. Arbitrary, unnatural divisions, such as *body and mind, space and time, person and environment*, lead to distinctions that do not correlate with the processes being described.
>
> *Two-value orientation*. The pronounced tendency to describe aspects of the world in terms of opposites, such as *black/white, big/little, old/ young, life/death*, leads to a vast number of either/or abstractions with few verbal symbols to represent intermediate conditions.
>
> *Allness orientation*. The tendency to perceive and describe the world in terms such as *every, never, always,* and *forever*, excludes convenient ways to qualify one's observations.

The direct implication of these flaws in the language structure is that they lead to "unsane" thought processes—distorted representations of the objective world. For example, if someone is prone to describe his experiences in either/or terms, he is likely to perceive the world that way, and he will expect to find either/or structures in his environment.

DISCUSSION

Significantly, the Structural Differential Model clarifies the relationship between verbal patterns and the process world they are intended to represent. The structural transitions that people make along the differential scale between the objective world-in-process and the internal world of verbal thought are revealed by the model. It focuses on the important transition from the world of "not-words" to the world of words. And it also calls attention to the "permanent et cetera," the idea that there is *always more* than can be perceived or described.

Primarily a cognitive model, the Structural Differential has its greatest utility in a learning situation when the group leader wants to focus attention on cognitive processes and problems of verbal communication. In this context, it is an extremely comprehensive discussion tool for either brief or protracted treatments of thinking and talking. From the model's description of the flaws of English, the group leader can explore ways of countering some of the pitfalls of language structure.

Because this is a process model, representing a flow of concepts rather than static relationships, its diagram is slightly more complex than many others. Consequently, the model is best developed by the group leader in cooperation with the group as a tool for guided discussion. If the diagram is drawn on a chalkboard or a newsprint pad, concept by concept, it can be kept in view during subsequent discussion. Presented in simple terms, with many examples from life, the model can capture attention and lead to a lively discussion of the relationships between language, thought, and behavior.

SUGGESTED READINGS

Bois, J. S. *Exploration in awareness.* New York: Harper & Row, 1957.

Chase, S. *The tyranny of words.* New York: Harcourt Brace Jovanovich, 1933.

Hayakawa, S. I. *Language in thought and action.* New York: Harcourt Brace Jovanovich, 1939.

Johnson, W. *People in quandaries.* New York: Harper & Row, 1946.

Korzybski, A. *Science and sanity: An introduction to non-Aristotelian systems and general semantics* (4th ed.). Lakeville, Conn.: Institute of General Semantics, 1958.

7 Lateral Thinking

The Lateral Thinking Model explains alternatives to conventional "patterned" cognitive processes. It incorporates some functional ways for capitalizing on the natural brain processes.

Edward De Bono, who introduced the lateral thinking concept, described the brain as (1) a self-organizing system and (2) a self-maximizing system. The first feature, self-organization, is the pronounced tendency of the brain to make sense out of the data provided to it by the sense organs. The brain seems to store information largely in patterns. Each bit of information entering the brain becomes a part of one or more patterns already stored in the brain. This means that an attempt to think about one isolated idea or image will bring with it a large amount of associated information. The more fully developed a cognitive pattern is, the more it tends to dominate thinking processes.

The second feature of brain functioning, self-maximization, operates to *confirm* certain patterns as information continues to flow into the brain. Once a pattern has developed, it begins to dominate not only the thinking processes, but the perceptual processes as well. The brain begins to *select* for recognition certain information that is compatible with the established patterns.

The effect of these two features of the brain's functioning is to create habits of thought that become entrenched. While a great number of these patterns are convenient and beneficial to the individual, e.g., control of routine mechanical functions and interpretation of standard signals, many others are self-defeating and dysfunctional. Certain patterns, which may be likened to beaten paths within the brain, tend to imprison the individual. They may bind him to a narrow range of options for dealing with his experiences.

The term *vertical thinking* describes the habitual style of thinking that is dominated by the brain patterns. Vertical thinking is logical and linear, e.g., if . . ., then; or cause and effect. It operates by establishing and following natural pathways, which link ideas together in ways consistent with the stored patterns.

The term *lateral thinking* describes a deliberate, conscious strategy for interrupting linear chains of thought. It does not destroy patterns, nor

36

does it operate without patterns. Instead, lateral thinking facilitates *transitions* between patterns, thereby widening the range of patterns available for dealing with a particular problem. Lateral thinking is also a strategy for creating new patterns that may be useful.

Associated with the strategy for lateral thinking are a number of specific techniques for putting it into operation. These include:

Free association: random association of ideas to discover relationships that were not previously known or appreciated; e.g., *computer* and *apple pie*;

Reversal: negation or inversion of a central idea or its implications to provide new perspectives; e.g., have the rabbit pull the magician out of the hat.

Distortion: exaggeration of specific features of known situations to provide new approaches or to clarify the influences of those features; e.g., make the bridge one thousand miles long;

Literalizing: association of an abstract, figurative word or phrase with its literal meaning—taking it at its "verbal face value"; e.g., design a clock that *tells* time by means of a recorded message;

Factoring: dissolution of inhibiting patterns by breaking them down into their component parts for repatterning; e.g., determining the smallest step involved in writing a book.

All of these methods for rearranging the elements of the problem and for developing new points of entry result in a wider range of alternatives available for consideration.

The vertical thinking process depends on sequential decisions, *all of which* must be correct for a useful result. If an individual has become imprisoned in the vertical thinking approach to a problem, he is not free to experiment with his thought processes. On the other hand, lateral thinking permits him to *abandon* the unsuccessful cognitive path. Although the jump may not be immediately successful, at the very least it frees the brain from the tyranny of the unsuccessful pattern.

Vertical thinking seems to be the primary mode of conscious thought in Western culture. This model represents lateral thinking as an appropriate adjunct to vertical thinking, not as a substitute for it. Lateral thinking as a strategy appears to be highly effective in improving application of the vertical processes. It capitalizes on known characteristics of the brain's methods of processing information.

The Lateral Thinking Model implies that creativity may not be, as commonly believed, strictly a gift or a genetic endowment; it is a strategical possibility available to everyone. If this is so, then creative thinking is a teachable skill, reducible to methods and techniques that one may learn, practice, and apply to practical problems.

Figure 7.1 compares vertical thinking with lateral thinking.

DISCUSSION

The Lateral Thinking Model has served well to stimulate creative problem solving. The model can be supported by many analogies and examples showing the limitations of vertical thinking. One such useful example is the well-known nine-dot problem, shown in Figure 7.2. The problem is to connect all nine dots with a continuously drawn line composed of four straight line segments. So strongly does the arrangement of the dots suggest a square, that very few people escape the inclination to confine the lines to an outer boundary. However, the solution, shown in Figure 7.3, is not constrained by the imaginary boundary.

The little nine-dot illustration powerfully demonstrates the brain's tendency to create patterns and make sense from its input, and, consequently, to impair and limit the individual's ability to reach solutions to problems. This concept can be extended from visual perception to more complex experiences, such as listening to others and reacting to unfamiliar situations and ideas. Other simple anecdotes from personal experience may be elicited from a group to enhance the presentation of this model.

Since the early 1940s, investigators have contributed ideas and techniques that seem to enhance creative thinking. The Lateral Thinking Model provides a useful framework for unifying these various techniques and for showing how they can be implemented.

SUGGESTED READINGS

De Bono, E. *The five-day course in thinking.* New York: Basic Books, 1967.
De Bono, E. *New think.* New York: Basic Books, 1968.
De Bono, E. *Lateral thinking: Creativity step by step.* New York: Harper & Row, 1972.

	VERTICAL THINKING	LATERAL THINKING
BASIC NATURE	Analytical Sequential Logical	Provocative Non-sequential Non-logical
PROCESS	Selective Converges toward acceptable solutions Use of negatives blocks certain paths Follows most likely path	Generative Seeks additional options Does not have to be correct to proceed Explores unlikely paths
USE OF PATTERNS	Retains labels, names, categories, and classifications from past experience	Attempts to escape from established patterns, labels, and classifications
RESULTS	Finite Predictable	Probabilistic Unpredictable

Figure 7.1. Comparison of vertical and lateral thinking

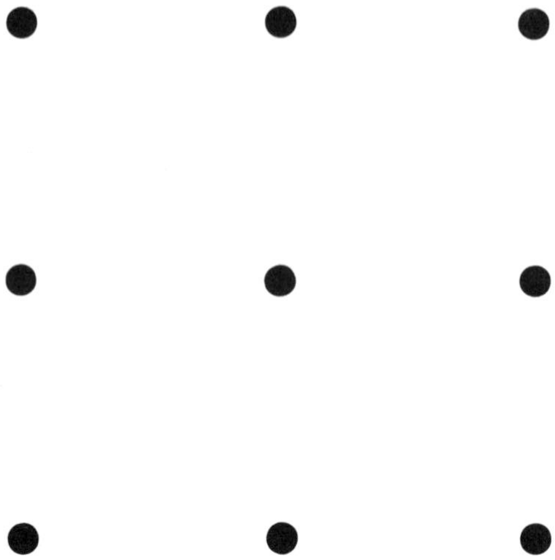

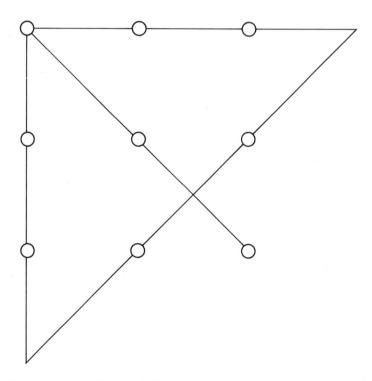

Figure 7.2. The nine-dot problem

Figure 7.3. The nine-dot problem solution

8 Accommodation of Feelings

Karl Albrecht formulated this model to interrelate three principal *styles* by which people come to terms with strong emotions. The model deals with thoughts and feelings, not as separable entities, as the either/or terminology implies, but as interconnected aspects of a person's responses to his experiences. Figure 8.1 shows a continuum as a linear range of possibilities for dealing with emotions.

At one extreme of the continuum, an individual can choose to *suppress* feelings as much as possible. That is, he resorts to various intellectual strategies that enable him to avoid dealing directly with his emotional reactions to the situation. He literally denies having any feelings.

At the other extreme, an individual may *capitulate* to his emotions, believing himself to be a helpless victim of feelings over which he has no control. He tends to assign responsibility for his happiness or unhappiness to external causes, such as other people or events.

The middle of the continuum represents the *accommodation* of feelings. The individual recognizes, accepts, and experiences emotions to bring about an integration of his feelings and his intellectual processes. These three styles of coping with emotions are expanded and interrelated in Figure 8.2.

The model applies particularly to the process by which an individual adapts to an emotional experience. Within the context of the model, an emotional experience is considered to be an event, positive or negative, to which an individual reacts with strong feelings. The assumption is also made that the individual can take it; that is, he does not psychologically disintegrate in response to the experience.

When he has an emotional experience, a person is faced with the problem of coping with his feelings and returning to a psychological equilibrium. This total process seems to obey a well-defined pattern, as shown in Figure 8.3.

The pattern seems to prevail for positive emotional experiences, as well as for negative experiences. Winning a large sum of money, unexpectedly being offered a very desirable job, or receiving a surprise award are examples of positive emotional experiences. Negative experiences would include the death of a loved one, loss of one's job, or sudden rejection by a person for whom one has a strong attachment.

Figure 8.1.   The intellectual-emotional continuum

STYLE	STRATEGIES	GENERAL CONSEQUENCES
SUPPRESSION	Denial of feelings Avoidance Rationalization Withdrawal	Emotional side effects of suppression Rigid patterns of interacting with others Feeling of detachment from peer groups Inability to form close and rewarding relationships
ACCOMMODATION	Recognition of feelings Acceptance of feelings Awareness of the process of adapting from an emotional disruption Facilitation of one's own adaptation	Reactions appropriate to the situation Understanding oneself and one's emotional responses Ability to form close and rewarding relationships Self-acceptance and high self-esteem Minimum time spent in helpless phase after emotional disruption Willingness to take emotional risks
CAPITULATION	Snap reactions Overreaction Blaming others for one's feelings "Insult shopping" Preoccupation with the events or conditions that gave rise to feelings	Feelings of helplessness Inability to maintain general equilibrium Low self-esteem Extreme susceptibility to the attitudes and opinions of others Inability to relinquish the past and plan for the future Dependency

Figure 8.2.   Styles of coping with emotions

43

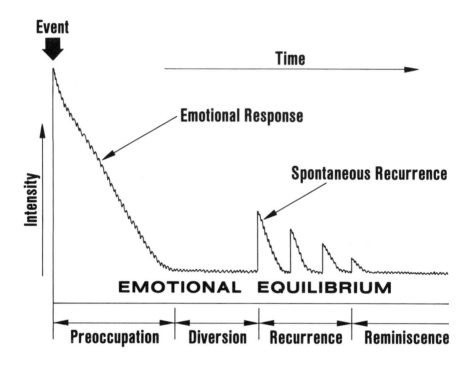

Figure 8.3.   Stages in recovery from a strong emotional experience

Figure 8.3 identifies the following four basic stages in the process of recovery from a strong emotional experience.

Preoccupation. During this initial phase, an individual's feelings are intense and he is strongly focused on the event or condition to which he has reacted. Almost hypnotized by the object of his feelings, he may be aware of, and unable to concentrate on, little else until the first emotional peak subsides. In this phase, his intellectual processes operate at a fairly primitive level.

Diversion. This intellectual phase is characterized by a return to the real world of practical matters. No one can remain continually in a state of emotional excitement. Sooner or later, feelings will subside and intellectual activity will predominate in guiding behavior. For example, shortly after the death of a loved one, the survivor must begin to consider practical matters such as funeral arrangements, etc. This intellectual phase provides temporary relief from the emotional intensity of the first phase.

Recurrence. After the primary intellectual processes of the diversion phase have been carried out, feelings are automatically reactivated. The recurrence phase is characterized by repetition, with progressively diminishing intensity, of the feelings of the first phase.

Intellectual and emotional activities alternate. The emotional episodes are often triggered by cues from the individual's environment that recall the event or condition to which he originally reacted. Eventually these feelings recur so infrequently, and with such little intensity of feeling, that they may be considered to be extinguished.

Reminiscence. The individual consciously recalls the event or condition that gave rise to the original feelings, but without the accompanying emotional arousal. This is primarily an intellectual activity. The feelings may be remembered but they are not re-experienced.

The nature of this process of recovering from an emotional experience varies with a number of conditions. Some of the more significant conditions are the *intensity* of the original experience, the availability of *options* for altering the disturbing conditions, and the presence of *distractions* that call for the individual's attention and shorten the duration of the preoccupation phase.

Many people do not move about within the intellectual-emotional continuum, but instead occupy a narrowly defined neighborhood on the line. A person who is accustomed to controlling his emotions has difficulty in capitulating to them, or even in accommodating them. And one who has developed the capitulation style is not likely to be able to suppress emotions or to accommodate them.

The Accommodation of Feelings Model offers an expanded range of options for coping with emotions. An individual who adopts the style of accommodation will quickly recognize the process that is taking place and will see himself as confronted with a recovery period. If the emotional experience is a positive one, he faces little challenge, unless some unusual circumstances dictate that he not appear to enjoy the emotions he is experiencing. For negative experiences, he will begin to recognize and accept his feelings and adopt a style commensurate with the constraints of the situation, usually some balance between suppression and capitulation. A person who has mastered the accommodation style has the option to navigate across the entire continuum, according to his basic strategies for living and the dictates of the situation.

DISCUSSION

Because it deals with both cognitive and emotional processes, the Accommodation of Feelings Model has a broad range of applications. It may be represented very simply with diagrams, and many of its implications are self-evident.

A primary value of the model is in focusing attention on *options* for coping with feelings. The group leader may find the model helpful in communicating with individuals who operate at either extreme on the continuum. Occasionally, we have found "encounter hobbyists," people who have learned to release emotions in the encounter setting, but who have not learned to integrate their emotions with their intellectual processes. The model can be useful in enabling such individuals to accept the role of cognitive processes in their adjustments to strong feelings.

The model can be introduced early in the group's life in order to establish a sense of direction and understanding of the experiences to come. Alternatively, the model can be introduced at a critical juncture in the group's development in order to prevent the group from leveling off at a point of preoccupation with feelings for their own sake.

The model also serves as an excellent tool for aiding re-entry to one's normal life environment, a common problem after intense experiential learning situations. It clarifies the need to reach the accommodation mode within the confines of the encounter setting in order to avoid problems associated with returning to the normal social or business environment.

9 Transcendence

The Transcendence Model brings into sharp perspective a broad range of possibilities for personal growth. The model, introduced by J. William Pfeiffer, identifies three distinct *states* or *levels* of individual growth.

Pfeiffer sees individuals as capable of moving from a state of *passive aggression (Level I)*, progressing through an *open expression* of hostility and other strong emotions *(Level II)*, and finally *transcending* to a more constructive response pattern, *introspective sharing (Level III)*. These three levels may be associated with *Dependence, Independence,* and *Interdependence* and can be diagrammed as shown in Figure 9.

Throughout childhood a person receives from others a multitude of direct and indirect messages about himself. From these messages, he develops both an image of himself and a perception of the way he is expected to behave. Frequently, these messages tell the individual that he is dependent and unworthy. The world is populated by people who are stronger, bigger, older, and more experienced and who exercise some degree of social, physical, or psychological authority. From these people, particularly in Western culture, come social norms that call for, among other things, suppression of strong emotion, politeness, respect for authority, etiquette, and modesty.

Dependency

Frequently, external forces tend to force the individual into a psychological and behavioral condition represented by Level I. It is characterized by patterned behavior, suppressed aggression, and low self-esteem.

Often, the norms enforced upon the individual are in conflict with his own preceptions and behavioral inclinations. From these conflicts he may develop guilt feelings that spur him to modify his behavior even more into conformance with the norms. He becomes locked in the dependency of Level I.

Independence

The dependent person may become aware of another more desirable condition, the independence of Level II. In the Level II position, the

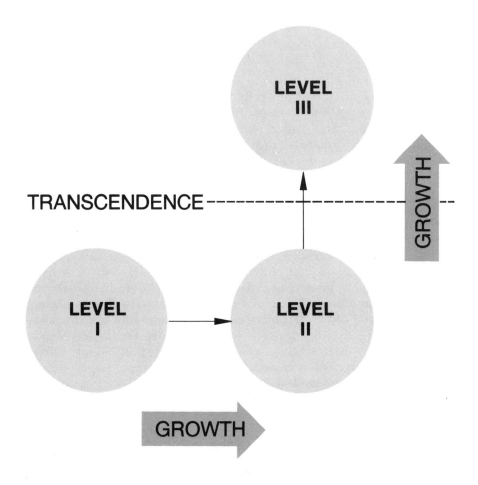

Figure 9. The concept of transcendence
(Adapted from Pfeiffer 1972)

individual frees himself of his former constraints, expressing his emotions freely. As he moves from dependence to independence, he is able to enhance his self-image in many respects. Regardless of the dictates of others, he is his own person, making his own decisions and acting upon them. He still engages in patterned behavior, but at another extreme.

Interdependence

Anxious to escape Level I, the individual may perceive Level II as a life style and be content with it. He may not be aware that he can *transcend* both dependence and independence to reach the interdependence of Level III, which allows him to enjoy the full potentials of both Level I and Level II positions.

Level III is characterized predominantely by the absence of the polar extremes of Level I and II behavior. In Level III, an individual becomes unlocked from his compulsions toward suppression or expression, dependence or independence. Free of patterned behavior of either type, he is able to share his feelings of anger, joy, and aggression with others and to share in their feelings. He is able to depend upon others and have them depend upon him in accordance with mutual needs and desires. He is able to develop a more "accurate" self-image, encompassing both good and bad feelings about himself.

An individual cannot move directly from Level I to Level III. The ability to deal effectively with strong emotions cannot come until the person has experienced and learned to cope with full expression. He cannot interact with others in an interdependent way until he has experienced and explored independence.

The model implies that communication is difficult between persons who are on different levels, because of their differing perspectives. Communications between individuals operating on Level I and Level III are extremely difficult, if not impossible. An individual who is bound by dependent behavior cannot share, and may even be frightened by, the needs or desires of Level III individuals.

DISCUSSION

The concept of *transcendence* is inherent in many other models about people. However, the Transcendence Model serves a valuable function by extracting a common idea and presenting it in a form that emphasizes processes and implications. It offers an alternative to either submitting to life's pressures or rebelling against them. Both of these positions tend to isolate people from each other. If the individual is able to reach Level III, he is able to interact in a much richer and more rewarding way with others.

Perhaps the most direct use of the Transcendence Model is in developing insight into the objectives of learning facilitators. Helping people to break free from Level I behaviors, and enhancing their ability to express strong emotions and act independently is only a part of the job. Wherever possible, facilitators must communicate the Level III concepts and attempt to aid an individual's transcendence.

In the academic environment, the model may provide insight into the essential characteristics of some other models. However, the model does lose some of its personal impact in the lecture-discussion format. Almost all models concerned with personal growth include an element of the idea of transcending from a behavior pattern that is dysfunctional to one that is more successful.

In the experiential learning environment, the model has substantial impact if the timing of its introduction is appropriate. There are at least two ways to use it. At the beginning of a session, it serves as a model for goal setting for the group. Later in the group process, it can be introduced when the group, in general, has progressed to Level II and is leveling off or becoming satisfied with its accomplishments. It can give impetus and direction to the group, as well as provide members with some insights into their status.

SUGGESTED READING

Pfeiffer, J. W. Transcendence theory. In J. W. Pfeiffer & J. E. Jones (Eds.), *The 1972 annual handbook for group facilitators.* La Jolla, Calif.: University Associates, 1972.

PART 2
DYAD MODELS

INTRODUCTION TO
DYAD MODELS

Two-person models, commonly referred to by behavioral scientists as *dyad* models, represent some of the most significant and interesting of human processes—face-to-face interactions. Dyad models are popular with facilitators, possibly because the models are relatively straightforward and because they provide a rich source of insight into human behavior.

Dyad models might be classified as a subclass of communication models, if the definition of communication is broad enough to include nonverbal as well as verbal processes. Many communication models portray a general class of interactions and could be considered a model. However, we prefer to operate at a more specific level of abstraction, using models that deal with more specific basic patterns, processes, and reactions—models that allow more useful inferences to be drawn.

Considerable caution is needed in extending individual-oriented models to circumstances involving two people. It is tempting to do this, but the processes represented by a dyad model are more than the juxtaposition of two individual processes. The behavior of one individual will be modified to some degree by the mere presence of another individual. In a dyad, each person becomes aware that he is interconnected with another, and has a wide choice of options for interacting with that person. Even withdrawal can be considered a form of interaction.

A fundamental concept underlying all two-person models is the "closed-loop" interaction process: A's behavior is in response to B's behavior, which was in response to A's behavior, and so on, endlessly. This is not to say that the behaviors of the two people are not strongly modified by other circumstances within their situation. But it does suggest a certain dynamic character to their interaction, which must be dealt with in some way. All the models in this section fulfill that requirement. Each offers its own unique approach to understanding two-person relationships. We consider these dyad models to be indispensable components of the facilitator's tool kit.

10 Ego-Behavior Distinction

One of the simplest of the dyad models, the Ego-Behavior Distinction Model, distinguishes between observed behavior and the inferences that are frequently made by the observer about the subject's internal *ego* functions.

The ego, as the term is used here, synthesizes a person's needs, attitudes, beliefs, opinions, feelings, and motives. These functions constitute the individual's *inner self*. They can never be known directly by the observer. They are internal—known only to the person. Many ego functions are "unverbal" in that they are not readily conceived or communicated by verbal language tools.

The observable aspect of the individual, his behavior, constitutes his *outer self*. It encompasses actions, gestures, physical habits, and mannerisms of speech and movement. This outer self is considered to be the physical manifestation of the inner self.

One of the principal causes of misunderstanding and faulty communication between two persons is the tendency to make inferences from observed behavior and to rely on them as accurately representing the individual's inner self, or ego. One example of this mistake might be the labeling of a very quiet person as "conceited." Since behavior can originate in a variety of ego characteristics, the person might have chosen to be quiet for any of several reasons. He may be very unsure of himself in a particular situation. If he is extremely lacking in self-esteem, he certainly would not be likely to tell everyone about it. Instead, he would probably adopt behavior strategies designed to persuade others that he is self-assured and self-sufficient. These strategies—bearing, posture, gestures, and perhaps a contrived silence—might be interpreted incorrectly by others as signs of conceit. Similarly, many people fail to see beyond the aggressive behavior of the loudmouth to the possibility that he might be very unsure of himself.

It is commonly assumed that a particular kind of behavior has a reason, a reason that is the same for all people and all circumstances. A more flexible approach would be to consider the behavior as but one element of a consistent pattern with which the individual expresses his ego, or internal make-up. This point of view requires careful consideration of an isolated element of behavior and a delay in drawing conclusions until more is known. If making an inference about a person's ego is necessary as a basis for one's own actions, then the inference should be recognized as tentative. In this way, it can be tested within the context of one's continued interactions with the other person.

Frequently in interpersonal relations, a person may consciously or unconsciously interpret someone else's behavior in terms of ego-behavior characteristics. For example, in the statement "Michael is avoiding me; he must not like me," the word "avoiding" represents an inference in itself. A more accurate observation might be "Michael hasn't spoken to me since we were first introduced to each other." This semantic strategy allows for the *hypothesis* "I wonder if he dislikes me?" And the hypothesis, in turn, may suggest a test such as "I think I'll walk over to his office and strike up a conversation with him." In this way, one can discover the actual ego-behavior relationships of the other person, instead of mixing one's own behavioral patterns into conclusions about him.

The Ego-Behavior Distinction Model offers a functional strategy for minimizing misunderstandings and conflicts that occur between two people. It suggests that an individual can enhance a relationship by communication information about his own ego functions and the other person's behavior. Figure 10 illustrates this strategy.

If a person talks about his own ego, *without regard to* the other person's behavior, he is said to be engaging in *disclosure*: "I sometimes worry about whether I'm really a worthwhile person." If he discusses his own ego *in relation to* the other person's behavior, he is engaging in *feedback* to the other person: "When you walk by without saying 'Hello,' I feel hurt."

The model proposes that feedback and disclosure are effective in developing and maintaining satisfactory interpersonal relationships. When an individual draws conclusions about the other person's ego ("You don't love me"), he is attributing ego characteristics that the person may feel are unwarranted. Such accusations are seen as personal affronts to the ego and must be defended against. This type of activity in a relationship is dysfunctional. The alternatives to accusation and evaluation are information seeking and information giving.

DISCUSSION

We have found the Ego-Behavior Distinction Model quite useful in revealing some causes of conflict and combativeness in interpersonal relations. It provides a clear strategy for improving a relationship.

It is not absolutely necessary that both persons in a dyadic relationship

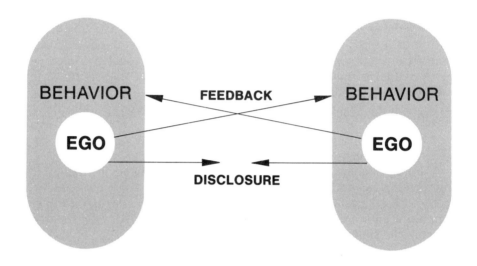

Figure 10. Ego-Behavior distinction in relationships.

understand the concept. If one party begins to implement this strategy for improving relations, he can see the results even if the other person is unaware of what is happening. Even though the strategy can be employed by one party in the relationship, it is essentially a nonmanipulative strategy.

In individual counseling, as well as in dyadic or group situations, this model provides a conceptual framework for getting to the source of the problem and gives a simple vocabulary for discussing actions for improvement.

This model first came to the attention of Walt Boshear in a team-building workshop that he was co-facilitating with Dr. Frank Jasinski in Nevada. Since that time, it has been adapted to fit our styles and needs. The occasion never arose for discussing the source of the model with Dr. Jasinski before his death in 1973. We have never encountered the model in any other situation and cannot provide any specific references for it.

11 Transactional Analysis

The Transactional Analysis Model, developed by Eric Berne, is one of the most comprehensive and useful tools available for dealing with interactions between two people. In this model, Berne assumes that each person has three possible ego states (patterned sets of thoughts and feelings): a Parent, an Adult, and a Child. (Note that the terms parent, adult, and child have specialized definitions in the vocabulary of transactional analysis.)[1] A dyadic interchange consists of *transactions* between the ego states of two people.

The Parent is, in one sense, the law-and-order ego state. It is the source of values, opinions, social conscience, rules and regulations, "shoulds" and "should nots," and "how-to" information. The Parent ego state also has a nurturing aspect when it guides, teaches, and advises. When in this state, the individual is behaving according to his value system.

The Adult is the unemotional, thinking ego state. When in this state, the individual collects information, weighs alternatives, tests reality, suggests hypotheses, and makes decisions. He also may exchange information or ideas with someone else. In particular, the individual does not experience any strong feelings in this state.

The Child is the "feeling" state. It is the storehouse of feelings and emotional reaction patterns from childhood. When in this state, the individual experiences strong feelings that are triggered by his immediate experiences.

Transactional analysis (TA) theory asserts that every person has all three ego states and switches from one to the other when interacting with others. The names of the ego states are not intended to imply that one state is better than another. For example, the Child state is not considered immature or undesirable. It merely denotes the behavioral pattern characterized by strong feelings. Similarly, the Parent state is neither good nor bad. It is simply a source of rules and regulations. The Adult state is not considered the ideal state, although it does examine and update data from the Parent and the Child to determine what is appropriate to the circumstances.

---

1. Ego states are also described in Model 2.

Transactions

When two people are interacting, each one may operate from any one of his three ego states. This means that there are nine possible *combinations* to consider when trying to understand transactions between two people. In TA theory a transaction is defined as a message originating in one ego state in one person and aimed at a particular ego state in another person. Figure 11 shows several of the more interesting transactions.

The *Parent-to-Child* transaction occurs frequently in dyadic exchanges. In this situation, one person has a psychologically superior position over the other, such as a real parent has over a real child. This might also be considered a differential in social power. The transaction will consist of a message, a statement, or a nonverbal signal from the superior person's Parent to the subordinate person's Child, or vice versa. An example might be a supervisor's statement to an employee: "Come into my office, Bob. I want to talk to you." This is a Parent-to-Child statement. If Bob feels Child-like, he will respond with statements or body language typical of the subordinate position. He may enter meekly, expecting to be chastised or rewarded by his supervisor.

The *Adult-to-Adult* transaction is the basis for conducting much of our day-to-day business. Typical Adult-to-Adult statements are: "What time is it?"; "Here's the report on the design study"; "I plan to take the car to the repair shop tomorrow"; and "I'd like you to meet my friend Tony."

The *Parent-to-Parent* exchange is usually a short-term interaction in which statements of opinion or values are exchanged, such as two people complaining about some social injustice or other. One person may say, "You just can't get good service any more." This is a Parent statement. The other person may respond with another Parent statement, such as "That's a fact. Why, I remember . . ."

The *Child-to-Child* exchange is a very important and interesting situation in which both parties experience strong feelings. These may be positive feelings associated with play, recreation, or just "horsing around." Sexual intercourse is likely to be a Child-to-Child interaction. An emotional argument is a Child-to-Child interaction on the negative side, one reason why a heated argument is so difficult for the two arguers to resolve. Each person, temporarily imprisoned in his Child state, is unable (or unwilling) to perform the rational thinking that is characteristic of the Adult state. When one (or both) of them returns to the Adult state, he perceives additional options for resolving the difficulty.

A fundamental concept of transactional analysis is that the Adult state is a mediator in the individual's interactions with others. If the person's three ego states are appropriately separated from one another, the Adult can serve as a general monitor of experiences and reactions. The Adult

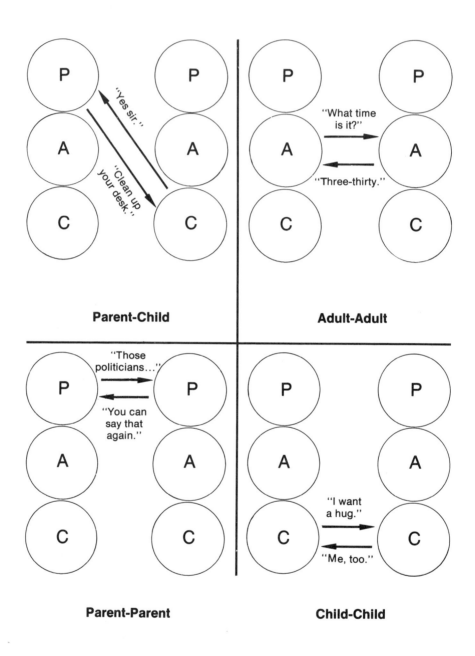

**Figure 11. Typical transactions between ego states
(Adapted from Berne 1964)**

prevents the individual from becoming angry or hurt by minor provo-
cations, and it enables him to acknowledge and experience his Child
feelings under appropriate circumstances.

Transactional analysis suggests that the individual can influence the
ego state of others, as well as his own. This process requires being aware
of one's own ego configuration, assessing that of the other person, and
adopting strategies to bring about the desired interaction. By observing
the actions of another and inferring his ego state, one can act or speak in
the way most likely to affect the other's ego state favorably.

DISCUSSION

The Transactional Analysis Model is useful and applicable to many different learning situations. It is a convenient lecture tool, allowing the lecturer to convey a number of significant concepts about human behavior
with considerable impact. It invites active participation in the seminar or
lecture-discussion environment. Either the seminar leader or participants
can offer many examples of recent transactions with family, friends, or
work associates. It is both interesting and useful to examine these real-life
experiences to determine the ego state from which both participants were
operating at the time of the transaction.

Even in relatively structured learning environments, people seem
willing to roleplay various interpersonal situations and then discuss the
simulated transactions in terms of the TA Model. Perhaps this is because
the model focuses on the observable *behavior* of the transaction, which is
relatively easier than wrestling with the more abstract *cause* of the behavior. Being able to label behavior as originating from "my Parent" or
"my Child" facilitates communication between participants and enables
them to move quickly to more functional behavior. There is less chance of
becoming bogged down in attempts to define "why" a person is engaged
in a certain type of behavior.

In experiential learning, which allows a norm to be established for
experimentation, the TA Model provides both a vocabulary and a meth-
odology for experiencing the results of different types of transactions. The
model is particularly useful for exploring the dynamics of boss-
surbordinate relationships in organizations, and it can provide a penetrat-
ing understanding of husband-wife (or couple) relationships.

Closely associated with the concept of transactional analysis are the
ideas of *strokes* and *contracts*. The stroke, recognition of the existence of
another person, is the unit of an interpersonal transaction. It may be
positive and pleasant or negative and unpleasant. Humans need strokes
from other people in order to survive. The individual who cannot get
positive strokes often will settle for negative ones. In conjunction with the

TA concept, the stroke concept is powerful. Participants in a learning group can gain practice in giving and receiving different kinds of strokes and in asking for and responding to requests for strokes.

The transactional contract is an agreement, usually unspoken, between people to interact with one another in certain patterned ways. There are one-stroke contracts, such as the "hello's" people exchange in passing, and multiple-stroke contracts, which can become very complex and involved. Analyzing these contracts by using the TA Model can lead to understanding and insights, which in turn can be applied toward new and more functional contracts.

SUGGESTED READINGS

Berne, E. *Transactional analysis in psychotherapy.* New York: Grove Press, 1961.

Harris, T. A. *I'm OK—You're OK: A practical guide to transactional analysis.* New York: Avon Books, 1973.

Meininger, J. *Success through transactional analysis.* New York: New American Library, 1974.

12 Multi-Channel Communication

Karl Albrecht formulated the Multi-Channel Communication Model to deal with blocks in communication that result when feelings, values, and opinions are confused with facts. Albrecht suggests that transactions between two persons take place through four separate communication channels that transmit *facts, feelings, values,* and *opinions,* as illustrated in Figure 12. Albrecht offers the following definitions:

Facts: objectively verifiable aspects of experience; inferences, conjectures, or assumptions that are believed to be true; information or data having no particular emotional connotation;

Feelings: emotional responses to experience; here-and-now reactions that influence the transaction;

Values: ideals; behavioral standards based on one's sense of propriety; relatively permanent ideas about what should be; experiences, people, concepts, or institutions that one holds dear;

Opinions: a belief or judgment that falls short of certainty and is oriented to the immediate situation; short-range ideas about what is happening, how others are behaving, what is being said or proposed; attitudes associated with a decisive stand or a position one has adopted.

All four kinds of information are exchanged to some degree in any dyadic interaction. Usually, one of them forms the predominant mode, but some trace of each of the others is always present. For example, in a typical business discussion, facts predominate. Feelings are involved to the extent that each person accepts the other, considers him to be competent and cooperative, and enjoys working with him. Values come into play throughout the transaction ("This project is worthwhile"). The two people have opinions that affect the decision issues ("I don't like this format for the report"), but their opinions continually shift in response to new information, re-evaluation of facts, and the influences of their relationship.

Person A

Person B

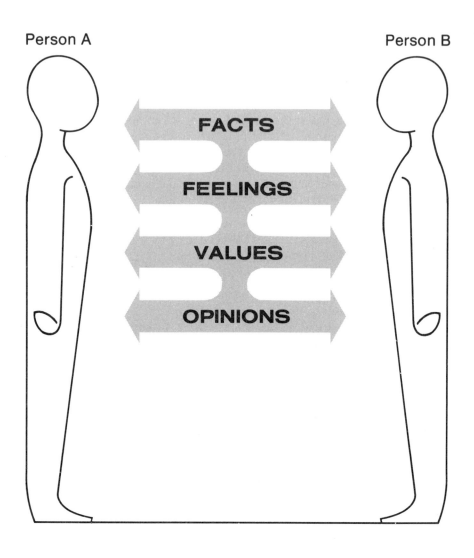

Figure 12. Multi-channel communications

Mixed Channels of Communication

The Multi-Channel Communication Model deals specifically with situations in which the four channels are inadvertently "mixed." Perhaps the most frequently mixed channels of communication are facts and opinions. For example, one person might say, "That's a stupid idea. It will never work." The language of his statement implies that the stupidity of the idea is a verifiable fact. In reality, however, he probably means "I don't like it. I disagree with the approach, and I believe it is unlikely to work."

A typical form of semantic maladjustment is the belief that "He realizes that is just my opinion." But unfortunately, the listener may not "hear" what was not said. He may react at the feeling level with a statement such as "You don't even understand the idea! You are not qualified to pass judgment on it!" Again, the statement seems to be coming across the *factual* channel, but it is laden with anger and frustration—strong *feelings* that are not being acknowledged. Needless to say, the immediate attitudes of the participants will heavily influence the course of the transaction, probably leading to further argument, exchanges of values and feelings that are expressed as facts, and increased hostility.

A fundamental principal of the Multi-Channel Communication Model is that *unrecognized* messages, conveying values, feelings, or opinions under the guise of "facts," exert subtle pressures on the listener. These are pressures to agree, to conform, to capitulate to the values of others, or to defend oneself against the aggressive feelings of others. It follows that being aware of each of these channels and separating them can lead to greater empathy, understanding, and consideration for the personal sovereignty of each person in the transaction.

The model implies that people are not capable of listening objectively—in fact each person sees and hears through a filter made up of his own values, feelings, attitudes, and reaction patterns. If the sender of a message assumes that the receiver can accept his message, can separate the facts from the sender's values, feelings, and opinions, and can react only to the facts, then the sender is very likely to be disappointed in his transactions with others.

Overcoming Blocked Communication

The first steps toward overcoming a communication block are to become aware of the four channels, to differentiate them, and to call attention to the confusion between them. This procedure is often referred to as *making a process statement*. For example, one might say, "George, you seem to be upset. Let's talk about that before we go any further. I want us to reach an agreement without hard feelings." This statement should bring George's feelings into the proper channel of communication. After being acknowledged in the conversation as legitimate feelings, they can be dealt with in such a way that George can return to the "factual" channel to complete the transaction.

Certain phrases, such as "to me," "up to a point," "so far as I know," "in my opinion," and "I feel" can be spectacularly effective in removing communication blocks. Such phrases call attention to the four channels of communication and separate them so they can be dealt with individually.

The Multi-Channel Communication Model also draws attention to body language (gestures, mannerisms, posture, etc.) as a medium for increased understanding. Although verbal communication is often unreliable for conveying true feelings and attitudes, the nonverbal mode is reliable if correctly interpreted.

In Anglo-Saxon cultures, denial of feelings and attitudes is so customary that many people automatically resort to rationalizing, intellectualizing, and diverting attention in order to conceal their feelings. Common statements heard in heated discussions are "Now, let's not get personal," or "Let's stick to business and not get our glands involved." Body language can be an extremely valuable asset for detecting inconsistencies between facts and feelings. For example, John's verbal message may be, "Gee, Fred, I'm really glad you came in to discuss this matter with me." But if John at the same time is glancing at his watch and standing by the door, then he is making quite another statement nonverbally.

DISCUSSION

The Multi-Channel Communication Model serves well to illustrate some causes of interpersonal misunderstanding. In the lecture-discussion environment, participants can recall recent conversations and describe the exchanged information in terms of the four channels. It is also useful for them to distinguish between verbal and nonverbal behavior and to note the types of information they transmit. For a less formal environment, a list containing a few examples of each of the four types of information can be distributed. Small groups of participants can be assigned to classify each of the statements into one of the four categories.

In the experiential learning situation, presentation of the model can evoke an understanding of the reasons people have difficulty communicating with one another. It also can set the stage for a structured experience that allows the participants to experience the four channels.

Multi-channel communication can be demonstrated in a "fish-bowl," or group-on-group experiment. Participants form two circles, one inside the other. While the inner group performs a task or interacts in some way, the people in the outer group observe the process, noting what channels of communication are used and how they are used. Following the activity, they discuss their observations; then the groups reverse roles.

An effective nonverbal activity can be developed from the model, identifying the most functional communication mode for each channel of information. Using only nonverbal techniques, such as gestures, facial expressions, and body position, each partner in a dyad attempts to communicate in turn: a fact, feeling, value, and opinion. While experimental in nature, such a structured experience is sufficiently nonthreatening to be used in some rather formal groups.

SUGGESTED READINGS

Keyes, K. S. *How to develop your thinking ability.* New York: McGraw-Hill, 1950.
Pietsch, W. *Human BE-ing.* New York: Lawrence Hill, 1974.

13 "Round" Ideas

The Round-Idea Model was developed by Walt Boshear as a convenient and entertaining tool for discussing the desirability of accepting "half-baked" ideas as subjects for serious discussion. Striking directly at the traditional concept of placing the responsibility for communication solely on the communicator, the model suggests a joint responsibility of the participants in a dialogue.

In most situations, a high value is placed on complete ideas and concepts—ideas with "straight edges and square corners." That is, if a statement is immediately perceived as being linked to other accepted ideas, it is accepted as a *building block*, and the speaker is rewarded for having the idea. However, if the idea cannot be perceived as a building block, the originator is punished by having his idea ignored. Many ideas and feelings are of this latter category. Boshear refers to them as "round" ideas—they "roll away" and are lost unless someone makes an effort to retain them.

To their originator, round ideas seem to be important and relevant, although he has not been able to "square them up" into building blocks. Boshear suggests that labeling these ideas as round can serve to "shore them up" and hold them in place while others examine them to see if they can be more fully developed. Incomplete ideas that are saved may be useful later in other circumstances.

The diagram in Figure 13 symbolizes the Round Idea Model. The geometric analogy can be extended to techniques for preventing round ideas from rolling away. If someone says, "Here's a round idea," he is asking his listeners to accept the idea temporarily and to avoid subjecting it to formal evaluation. This would amount to creating a "flat spot" on the idea, allowing it to come to rest for the time being. Later, he may be able to offer other fragmentary ideas that might supply "corners" for the idea, or a few questions from his listeners may help him to clarify his mental processes. If neither approach works, the idea is put into mental storage, perhaps to be considered again, perhaps not.

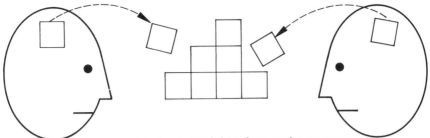

Ideas need to have *straight edges* and *square corners* to be immediately useful as *building blocks.*

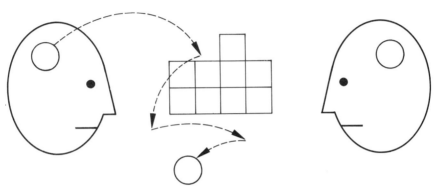

Some potentially valuable ideas are seen as *round.* They have no immediate use as building blocks and frequently *roll away.*

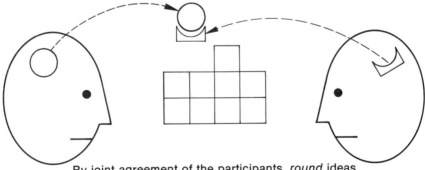

By joint agreement of the participants, *round* ideas can be identified and temporarily *shored up* for detailed examination and *squaring up.*

Figure 13.   The "round" ideas concept

DISCUSSION

At the heart of the Round Idea Model is the conviction that ideas have intrinsic value, although this value may not be perceived immediately. Ideas are the intellectual wealth of a problem-solving group. New and immature ideas, or ideas that are difficult to verbalize, are killed or crippled so routinely in the course of human affairs that any technique that preserves and nurtures them can be valuable.

We have found the model to be extremely useful, not only in learning situations, but as a tool of communication between us. In lectures on creative thinking and problem solving, the model serves as a simple way to deal with nurturing ideas in a light vein. In seminar situations, it is an effective prelude to practical experiences in brainstorming.

In the growth or encounter group environment, the model provides participants with a vocabulary to communicate preverbal feelings, attitudes, and intuitions—along with a process for handling them. Either the originator or the recipient of an idea can label it round, eliminating the ego threats that are implied by the customary descriptions of such ideas as incomplete, immature, confusing, or unclear.

14 Proxemic Zones

The Proxemic Zone Model of nonverbal communication delineates the social significance of the space surrounding a person's body. Each person perceptually structures his own spatial field into several zones of varying intensities. The presence of another individual within one of these zones has certain effects on the attitudes and actions of the "owner" of the territory.

Figure 14 illustrates the four principal zones that are recognized in the study of nonverbal communication.

Intimate Zone

The range of the *intimate zone* is defined by one's culture. In Western culture, for example, the intimate zone typically extends six to twelve inches outward from the body. It is usually reserved for personal friendship or sexual intimacy. The owner of the territory may react to an unauthorized intrusion into this zone with defensive feelings, avoidance behavior, and, sometimes, even with hostility.

Personal Zone

For Americans, the *personal zone* extends outward from the edge of the intimate zone to about an arm's length. This probably explains the American figure of speech "keeping him at arm's length." In some cultures, notably Mediterranean, the personal zone is smaller than this. For a Greek or an Italian, a friend standing at a distance of an arm's length would seem too distant for comfortable interaction. Entrance into an individual's personal zone is usually by invitation only.

Social Zone

From the edge of the personal zone, an individual's *social zone* extends outward to a distance determined by his environment. In a quiet office, the social zone might extend as much as twenty feet. In a noisy or crowded situation, the social zone might be as short as six to eight feet. When a person becomes aware of another individual within his social zone, he generally feels inclined to interact with that person in some way.

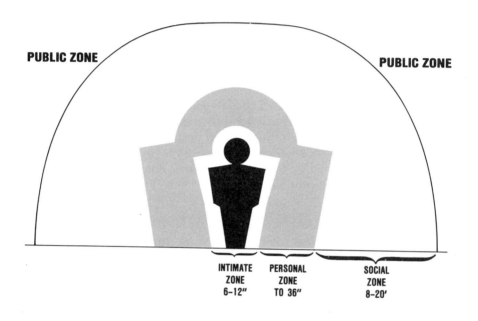

PUBLIC ZONE　　　　　　　　　　　　　　　　　**PUBLIC ZONE**

INTIMATE ZONE 6–12″　PERSONAL ZONE TO 36″　SOCIAL ZONE 8–20′

Figure 14. Proxemic zones

Public Zone

A *public zone* extends indefinitely outward from the edge of the individual's social zone. People within a person's public zone usually do not exert significant influence on his nonverbal behavior. They are perceived as undifferentiated aspects of his environment, usually requiring no special attention from him.

Body Language

The idea of *body language* (kinesics) is very closely connected with the concept of proxemic zones. A person's nonverbal messages—posture, gestures, movements, sounds, etc.—usually will express his attitudes toward the presence of others within his spatial zones. For example, he may react to an uninvited intrusion into his personal zone by backing away, turning aside, avoiding eye contact, or being apparently preoccupied with some distraction. Two people who are engaged in a stand-up conversation often will turn so that the fronts of their bodies form a right angle. This enables them to control the level of personal involvement quite precisely.

If stranger A is placed within the personal zone of individual B, then B will usually adjust his body configuration. For example, on a crowded bus, rider B will probably keep his face and torso oriented away from intruding stranger A. Rider B may preoccupy himself with anything from reading a book to picking imaginary lint from his sleeve. His nonverbal signals say to intruder A, "I accept your presence, but I do not intend to interact with you in any significant way." The intruding person will probably transmit many of the same signals. If the two should decide to engage in conversation, their nonverbal signals are likely to change, reflecting their increased relaxation and acceptance of more involvement.

Perhaps the most interesting study of body language centers on two-person and small-group interactions within the social zone. This is the space in which a great deal of business is transacted. It is also the zone in which casual social interactions occur. People in a business conference usually are within social distance of one another. However, participants who are sitting side by side might share their personal zones while they confer quietly on some topic or other. The side-by-side geometry makes the close proximity acceptable. At a family gathering or a quiet party in someone's living room, people will also be within social distance of one another.

The study of kinesics and proxemics offers abundant resources for interpreting nonverbal signals between people who are interacting at a social distance. General body position, posture, movements, gestures, and small mannerisms can be observed and interpreted to gain knowledge about the feelings and attitudes of individuals. And this knowledge can be used to facilitate one's own communication with others. By adopting certain nonverbal patterns, one can help others to relax, open up to communication, and increase empathy. One can also compare a person's nonverbal messages with his verbal statements to determine whether he is holding back, concealing information, or trying to mislead.

DISCUSSION

The four proxemic zones represent attitudinal and behavioral regions, rather than measurable aspects of the human body. In this regard, they should not be considered universal or invariable for any one individual. Each person's behavior is shaped by many factors other than proxemic zones.

One can observe an individual and make some assessment of his general patterns of relating to others on physical terms. However, it is important to include factors such as the presence of a large number of people, the general physical environment, noise level, social setting, and physical peculiarities of the individuals involved. For example, when a short person is interacting with a tall person, the short person's personal zone might be larger than it would be if he were dealing with someone of his own height. Many tall people are unaware that a difference in height intimidates some shorter individuals, causing them to seek a larger personal zone from which to interact.

We have found the Proxemic Zone Model to be most useful in lectures on nonverbal communication, as well as in seminars and workshops. It serves as an effective discussion tool for a group and lends itself easily to personal experience. In a workshop setting, each participant can react to the entry of another person into his various spatial zones.

The model also serves as a conceptual foundation for the design of structured experiences aimed at nonverbal awareness. For example, experiences such as two-person "sculpturing" (Pfeiffer & Jones, 1973, p. 21) serve as safe ways for one person to experience another within his personal zone. In a growth group setting, the model can help participants to understand their personal reactions to nonverbal interaction and to respect the spatial fields of others.

In our work in human relations training, we emphasize the role of nonverbal communication because an awareness of the basic dynamics of nonverbal interaction can be a valuable asset to almost anyone.

SUGGESTED READINGS

Birdwhistell, R. L. *Introduction to kinesics.* Louisville, Ky.: University of Louisville Press, 1952.

Fast, J. *Body language.* New York: M. Evans, 1970.

Hall, E. T. *The hidden dimension.* New York: Doubleday, 1966.

McKeown, L. A., Kaye, B., McLean, R., & Linhardt, J. Sculpturing: An expression of feelings. In J. W. Pfeiffer & J. E. Jones (Eds.), *A handbook of structured experiences for human relations training* (Vol. IV, Rev.). La Jolla, Calif.: University Associates, 1973.

Nierenberg, G. I. & Calero, H. H. *How to read a person like a book.* New York: Pocket Books, 1973.

Schnapper, M. Nonverbal communication and the intercultural encounter. In J. E. Jones & J. W. Pfeiffer (Eds.), *The 1975 annual handbook for group facilitators.* La Jolla, Calif.: University Associates, 1975.

15 Fundamental Interpersonal Relations Orientation (FIRO)

In the FIRO Model, William C. Schutz describes interpersonal relations in terms of basic needs for *inclusion, control,* and *affection*. He differentiates in each of these areas between the behavior and feelings we *express* toward others and the behavior we *want* from others.

A person will express these basic needs in varying degrees by attempting to interact or associate with others (Inclusion), to control or influence others (Control), and to demonstrate love and affection for others (Affection). Conversely, each person wants others to behave toward him by interacting or associating with him, by controlling or influencing him, and by showing love and affection for him.

The basic FIRO model has two dimensions that intersect with each other:

Inclusion/Control/Affection

Expressed Behavior/Wanted Behavior.

Figure 15 shows the six areas, or cells, of intersection that are created. In each of the cells is a statement representing an individual's orientation toward interpersonal relations.

To complete the basic FIRO model, Schutz added a third dimension to each cell—*intensity*. Intensity level describes the *degree* to which an individual expresses behavior toward others or wants them to express behavior toward him in each of the three areas (inclusion, control, affection). Extreme characteristics of people in each of the orientation modes are described by Schutz.

Inclusion

An *undersocial* person, at the extreme, withdraws from people. He does not attend social functions, nor will he initiate social activities and invite others to join him. At a lesser extreme, the undersocial person shows reluctance toward social activities—he may make a habit of arriving late or leaving early.

The *oversocial* person shows a strong need to be with others whenever possible. Seldom alone, he is both a joiner and an organizer. At the

	INCLUSION	CONTROL	AFFECTION
EXPRESSED BEHAVIOR (Toward Others)	I join other people I include others	I take charge I influence people	I get close to people
WANTED BEHAVIOR (From Others)	I want people to include me	I want people to lead me	I want people to get close and personal with me

Figure 15. The basic FIRO model
(Adapted from Schutz 1973)

extreme, he will be compulsive about having someone with him at all times. A more moderate position is indicated by an individual's attempts to be noticed. Whether the result is positive or negative, having people pay attention to him is what counts.

If a person has resolved his needs for inclusion he is able to be *social*. He is flexible in his relations, feeling comfortable either alone or with others. If he desires, he may be very involved in certain social activities and decline to participate in others.

Both undersocial and oversocial behaviors result from a poor self-image. The person who feels that others consider him unimportant may become either introverted ("I'm no going to risk being ignored") or extroverted ("I'll make people pay attention to me any way I can"). The social orientation requires a high self-image—a feeling of worth and identity.

Control

The characteristic behavior of the *abdicrat* is to avoid taking responsibility at any cost. He tends to associate with people who will take charge, allowing him to take a subordinate role.

The *autocrat* always wants to be in control. He may express this need directly, by attempting to dominate people, or indirectly, by attempting to gain prominence in sports, politics, or business—seeking a superiority that allows him to exercise control over people and situations.

The *democrat* is able to take either a dominant or subordinate role with equal comfort. He bases his assumption of control on its appropriateness to the current situation.

Schutz says that both abdicrat and autocrat behaviors represent the extreme reactions to feelings of incompetence. The abdicrat defers to strength in others, and the autocrat attempts to prove himself by always taking control. The person who feels competent (at least in some areas) is not driven to compulsive behavior in either direction.

Affection

A person who tends to avoid personal relationships with others, not wanting to get emotionally involved, is *underpersonal*. He may associate with others, but he keeps them at a distance. Rather than make individual distinctions between people, he probably will treat them all the same.

The *overpersonal* individual always needs to establish deep personal relationships. Not satisfied with acquaintances, he must be friends with everyone. The overpersonal person may be direct, affectionate, and intimate. More indirectly, he may be possessive and try to punish any attempts by his friends to establish other friendships.

When a person exhibits the ability to be comfortable either with intimacy or without emotional attachment, he is *personal*. He can accept the fact that he is liked by some and not by others.

Affection-oriented behavior is the result of a person's feelings about his lovableness. If he feels unlovable, he will be either underpersonal or overpersonal. If, on the other hand, he is secure in knowing that he is lovable, he can exhibit genuine affection with some people and be perfectly at ease with more impersonal relations with others.

Anxiety

Schutz's model can also provide some insight into certain types of anxiety. He described two situations, or potential situations, that produce anxiety: too much activity and too little activity. Anxiety can be viewed as a person's anticipation of situations in which he will:

be ignored or insignificant;

not be influential;

not be loved;

be enmeshed or denied privacy;

have too much responsibility; or

be smothered by affection.

DISCUSSION

As its name implies, the principal usefulness of the FIRO Model is in the area of interpersonal relations. But experience has demonstrated that the model is quite valuable in helping the individual to understand himself as well.

In the form presented here, the FIRO Model applies predominantly to normal interpersonal relations. The three types of behavior in each area represent a segment of the normal spectrum of behavior and feelings. It is possible, however, to extend Schutz's model into the realm of pathological behaviors (extreme anti-interactive and compulsive-interactive), but it requires a fuller interpretation and expansion of the model. The basic model is more than broad enough, however, to cover most interpersonal relations encountered in the training and counseling environment.

The FIRO Model is deceptively simple in appearance. Although it is not apparent on first examination, the model provides a framework for defining and discussing literally billions of distinct and different intrapersonal and interpersonal relationships. The concepts are fairly straightforward and not difficult to grasp. In very short order, the FIRO Model can be presented and a common terminology established. From this base, many real-life situations can be discussed with unusual depth.

In the lecture-discussion training situation, the FIRO Model requires only a short span of time for passing on large quantities of information about human relationships. Presented early in the session, the model can provide a base for later discussions. And it can serve the facilitator in much the same capacity in nonstructured or experiential learning groups.

SUGGESTED READINGS

Kormanski, C. L. Party conversations: A FIRO role play. In J. E. Jones & J. W. Pfeiffer (Eds.), *The 1975 annual handbook for group facilitators.* La Jolla, Calif.: University Associates, 1975.

Ryan, L. R. *Clinical interpretation of the FIRO-B.* Palo Alto, Calif.: Consulting Psychologists Press, 1970.

Schutz, W. C. *FIRO: A three-dimensional theory of interpersonal behavior.* New York: Holt, Rinehart and Winston, 1958.

Schutz, W. C. Fundamental interpersonal relations orientation—Behavior. In J. W. Pfeiffer, R. Heslin & J. E. Jones, *Instrumentation in human relations training* (2nd ed.). La Jolla, Calif.: University Associates, 1976.

Schutz, W. C. FIRO-B and FIRO-F. In J. W. Pfeiffer, R. Heslin & J. E. Jones, *Instrumentation in human relations training* (2nd ed.). La Jolla, Calif.: University Associates, 1976.

16 Open/Closed Relationships

The Open/Closed Relationships Model, developed by William Barber, characterizes open and closed relationships as extremes on a continuum. The degrees of openness or closedness in a relationship depend on how the two people handle four elements: the topic of conversation, the time frame of the topic, feelings, and personal information. Figure 16 illustrates the basic concepts of the model.

A Closed Relationship

A closed relationship, as implied by the diagram, can be characterized as a very superficial relationship. Neither of the persons is especially involved or interested in the topics of conversation. Most discussion concerns events that happened a long time ago or may happen in the distant future—or not at all. Both persons avoid having their feelings become an issue. If feelings begin to evidence themselves, both individuals are likely to become even more distant and abstract to avoid recognizing or discussing feelings or being personally involved. If personal topics are approached at all, they are likely to be abstracted and generalized to the point that neither participant "owns" them.

An Open Relationship

At the other end of the continuum, the open relationship is much more direct, varied, and expressive. The topic of discussion frequently is the relationship itself—what it is and how it is progressing. The subjects of discussion often concern "what is going on right now." Immediate experiences are shared as they are experienced, and feelings are a legitimate subject of discussion. The sharing of feelings is seen as an aid to communication and understanding. The participants become personally involved with one another, sharing private information, thoughts, feelings, and attitudes.

By representing open and closed relationships on a continuum, the model suggests that movement from one extreme to the other need not be revolutionary but can be evolutionary. By gradually changing the four elements of the relationship, the participants can move toward a more

81

CLOSED ←			→ OPEN
TOPIC			
Of concern to neither	Of concern to one	Of concern to both	The relationship
TIME FRAME			
None	Distant past or future	Recent past or future	Now
FEELINGS			
Excluded, Detractive		Included, Relevant	
PERSONAL			
Abstractions, Generalizations		Real, Private, Personal	

Figure 16. Open/Closed relationships
   (Adapted from Pfeiffer and Jones 1973)

open relationship—learning to take personal risks at a mutually acceptable rate. They also have the entire spectrum of relationships available to
them. Rather than make an either/or choice, they can move freely along
the continuum as appropriate to their purpose and circumstances.

DISCUSSION

We have found the Open/Closed Relationships Model extremely useful in
dispelling some of the fear associated with established open relationships
in group situations. People who come to a growth or encounter group
from a background of relatively closed relationships may have a distorted
view of their alternatives. It is not uncommon for such people to see the
open relationship as a dramatic jump from their previous behavior. This
model provides a clear transitional process through which an individual
can proceed at his own pace.

A useful feature of the model is that it can lead directly into the
formation of dyads for experiencing open and closed relationships. The
diagram, sketched on newsprint or as a handout, serves the participants
as a guide to the subjective assessment of their relationships as it pro-
gresses. It furnishes a vehicle and a vocabulary for moving a topic toward
the open end of the continuum. In this respect, the model is self-
reinforcing. As the dyads use the model to "take a small step" toward
openness, their experiences tend to increase their faith in the model. This
reinforced credibility of the model provides a basis for taking more personal risks. Not only does the model serve to clarify the ongoing process,
but when used in this manner, it *becomes part of the process*.

This model also appeals to us because it gives the group members a
practical tool for exercising their options in "back-home" interpersonal
relationships.

SUGGESTED READING

Building open and closed relationships. In J. E. Jones & J. W. Pfeiffer (Eds.), *The 1973
annual handbook for group facilitators*. La Jolla, Calif.: University Associates, 1973.

17 The Johari Window

Joe Luft and Harry Ingham developed the Johari Window Model (Joe + Harry = Johari) to clarify the definitions and functions of *feedback* and *self-disclosure*. In any interpersonal relationship, people give information and receive information. The nature of that information is determined by past relationships between the people and it, in turn, determines the nature of their future relationship.

The Johari Window Model offers a process for knowing ourselves and others better. As depicted in Figure 17.1, the model is a matrix—a two-dimensional table arranged in rows and columns representing the exchange of information in a relationship. The matrix resembles a window—a window through which each person gives and receives information about himself and others. The areas, or panes, of the window represent the totality of information about one's self available for sharing. For convenience, the areas of information contained in the Johari Window are described in the first person form:

The Public Self. The first pane contains knowledge about myself that I know and that others know. This may be information about my feelings and attitudes that I have shared with others, or it may be my observable behavior.

The Blind Self. The second pane reveals certain things that other people know about me that I do not know myself. I have mannerisms and other aspects of behavior of which I am unaware. People gain information about me directly or by inference from these behaviors.

The Private Self. In pane three are all manner of things that I know about myself but do not choose to share. For many reasons I withold this information about myself from others.

The Unknown Area. The last pane represents information about me that neither I nor anyone else knows. This information area may include my motivations, unconscious needs, and anxieties. Although soliciting and giving feedback can move the window panes' boundaries and reduce the unknown, there will probably always be an area of the unknown.

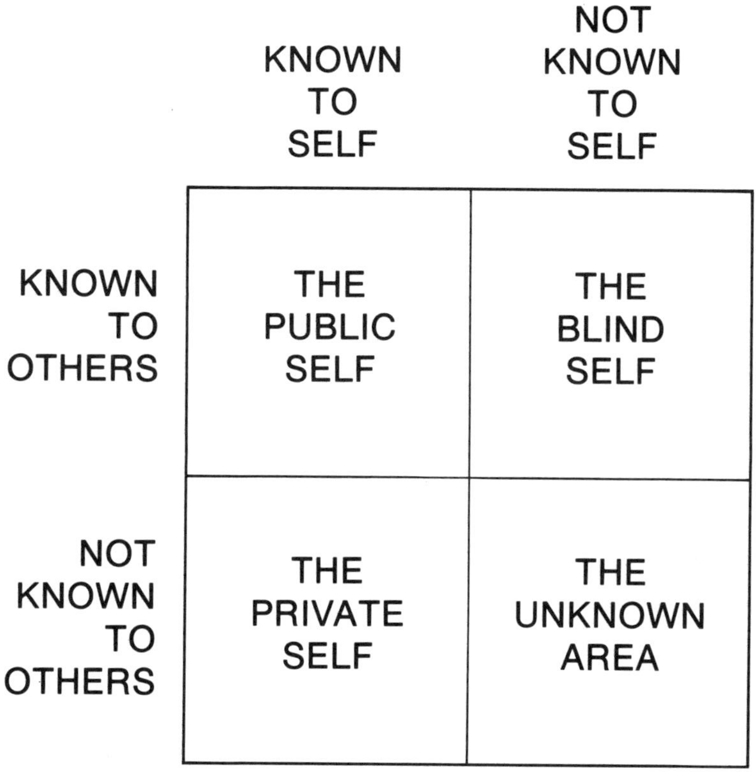

NOT
KNOWN
TO
SELF

KNOWN
TO
SELF

KNOWN
TO
OTHERS

THE
PUBLIC
SELF

THE
BLIND
SELF

NOT
KNOWN
TO
OTHERS

THE
PRIVATE
SELF

THE
UNKNOWN
AREA

Figure 17.1.   The Johari window model
(Reprinted from *Group Processes: An Introduction to Group Dynamics* by Joseph Luft, by permission of Mayfield Publishing Company. Copyright © 1963, 1970 by Joseph Luft.)

Disclosure and Feedback

The Johari Window Model clarifies the two important concepts of disclosure and feedback.

Disclosure occurs when one person trusts another enough to reveal aspects of himself that the other person does not know. The more he trusts, or the more he is willing to take risks, the more a person tends to disclose about himself. In terms of the model, he is decreasing the area of the Private Self and increasing the area of the Public Self, as shown in Figure 17.2.

Feedback occurs when people perceive that a person is receptive, and they share with him information that he does not know about himself. The more they see that he is open and interested in making constructive use of the information, the more they tend to take risks and reveal the impact he has on them. To the extent that feedback takes place, the person is able to reduce the area of the Blind Self, as shown in Figure 17.3.

In situations where there is high trust and a willingness to take risks, the area of the Public Self is enlarged by both feedback and disclosure, as shown in Figure 17.4.

The model identifies trust as an environmental condition for encouraging disclosure and feedback. It also implies that trust is built by taking risks and engaging in disclosure and feedback and that increased disclosure and feedback will enhance an interpersonal relationship.

DISCUSSION

The Johari Model is an excellent tool for clarifying the concepts and functions of feedback and disclosure. We feel this is the most powerful use of the model.

Since the introduction of the model, it has been extended and modified in various ways. However, attempts to extend the model's scope have, for us, only diluted its basic power and have tended to confuse rather than to clarify. We emphatically caution the reader to be wary of the "geometric" malfunctions that can result from these manipulations. For example, in one modification of the Johari Window Model, *disclosure* and *gives feedback* are equated along one dimension of the model. This distortion of the model is subtle, but it obscures the distinction between the two different functions.

Another modification represents attempts to measure the degree to which a person engages in feedback or disclosure. The two dimensions of the model are converted into a continuum with several gradations, as shown in Figure 17.5. The two intersecting lines are manipulated to describe the degree to which a person solicits feedback or engages in

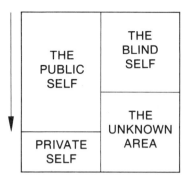

Figure 17.2.   The Johari model under conditions of disclosure

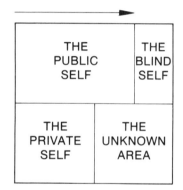

Figure 17.3.   The Johari model under conditions of feedback

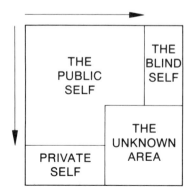

Figure 17.4.   The Johari model under conditions of disclosure and feedback

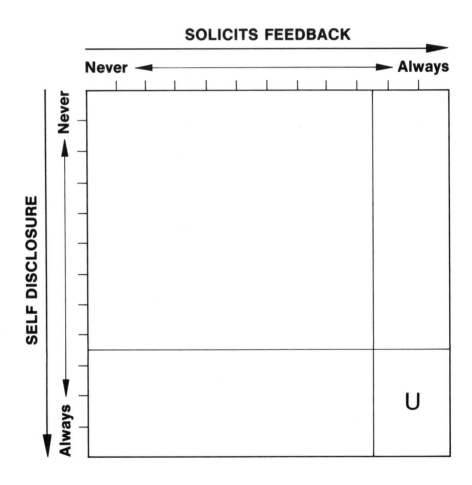

Figure 17.5.   Measuring feedback and disclosure

self-disclosure. The model implies, at least *visually*, that the Unknown Area is increased or decreased directly as a result of the amount of feedback one solicits or the degree to which he engages in self-disclosure. This distortion raises problems for which the model was not designed.

The Johari Window Model has the most impact in its original form. It is a simple visual aid for explaining the concepts of disclosure and feedback, either in a cognitive or experiential learning environment. If a situation calls for a deeper discussion of content, process, or measurement of disclosure and feedback, other models are more useful.

SUGGESTED READINGS

Hall, J., & Williams, M. Personnel relations survey. In J. W. Pfeiffer & R. Heslin, *Instrumentation in human relations training*. La Jolla, Calif.: University Associates, 1973.

Hanson, P. C. The Johari window: A model for soliciting and giving feedback. In J. E. Jones & J. W. Pfeiffer (Eds.), *The 1973 annual handbook for group facilitators*. La Jolla, Calif.: University Associates, 1973.

Luft, J. *Of human interaction*. Palo Alto, Calif.: National Press Books, 1961.

√ Luft, J. *Group processes: An introduction to group dynamics*. Palo Alto, Calif.: National Press Books, 1963.

Luft, J. Johari window: An experience in self-disclosure and feedback. In J. W. Pfeiffer & J. E. Jones (Eds.), *A handbook of structured experiences for human relations training*, Vol. I. La Jolla, Calif.: University Associates, 1969.

18 Transactional Games

Developed from Eric Berne's transactional analysis, the Transactional Games Model portrays a highly patterned and socially dysfunctional form of interplay between individuals. The transactional *game* is a sequence of person-to-person messages or transactions that result in a psychological "win" for the initiator of the game and a "loss" for the other, unwitting player.

The transactional game represents one level of involvement between two people on a more or less continuous range of possibilities. Berne divided this range into six general clusters, characterized by the intensity of involvement and the behavior typical of each. These six stages of involvement are Withdrawal, Rituals, Pastimes, Activities, Games, and Intimacy. Figure 18.1 summarizes the activities associated with each of these stages of involvement.

The model employs a concept from transactional analysis—the three ego states of individual personality, the Parent, Adult, and Child. (An ego state is a pattern of thoughts and feelings.)[1] The Parent ego state is characterized as providing a person's moral, social, and personal values, as well as traditional behavior guidance. The Adult ego state performs the data-gathering, analyzing, and reality-testing functions. The Child ego state represents the emotional characteristics of a person and provides the basic feelings. An individual occupies one or another of these ego states in all of his transactions with others.

The manner in which ego states are used to analyze a game is diagrammed in Figure 18.2. The arrows indicate the originator of each "message" in the game and the ego state of the receiver to whom the message is directed. The game diagrammed here is called "Kick Me." (Whimsical titles for games are characteristic of this theory.)

The numbered arrows in Figure 18.2 represent the individual messages in the time sequence of the game cycle:

1. Message number one, "Tell me you love me," is person A's *offer to play the game*. This message is directed from A's Child state to B's Parent

---

1. Ego states are also described in Models 2 and 11.

LEVELS OF INTERPERSONAL INVOLVEMENT

LEVEL	TYPICAL BEHAVIOR
Withdrawal	Physical departure from a threatening situation Psychological withdrawal if physical departure is not feasible Silence, preoccupation, pretending to be not there
Rituals	Standard behavior Discussions or conversations that deal with information known to both parties Social rituals such as greeting, leave-taking, and small talk Ceremonies, highly structured group behavior (plays, weddings, funerals, etc.)
Pastimes	Killing time, small talk, light conversation, recreation (e.g. sports, card games, etc.)
Activities	Task-oriented processes The basic business of living Carrying out business activities, commerce, social activities, meeting social obligations Communicating, negotiating, working together
Games	Complex interpersonal transactions Statements about each other, rather than about processes Subtle psychological attacks, diversions and NOT OK feelings
Intimacy	Sense of privacy, physical contact Pleasurable stroking, nurturing, and being nurtured In some situations, sexual arousal and/or intercourse

Figure 18.1. Levels of interpersonal involvement

"KICK ME"—A GAME

Situation: A very formal dinner party.

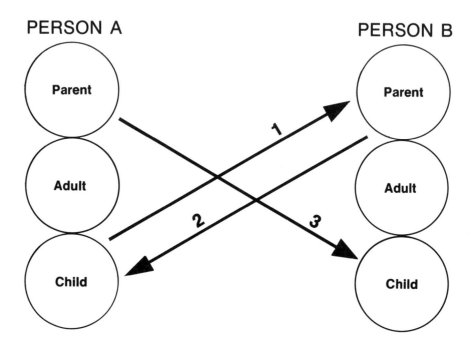

MESSAGE	PERSON
1. "Tell me you love me."	(A)
2. "Stop making a scene."	(B)
3. "You never show any affection! You only care about yourself!"	(A)
– ("I feel guilty.")	(B)
– ("Take that, you bum!")	(A)

The transactional game process.
(Adapted from Berne 1964)

state. It is the beginning of a *setup*, because A realizes that the highly formal situation—a dinner party—will probably constrain B from giving the requested response, or "stroke."

2. Person B *accepts the game* and responds with message number two, "Stop making a scene." This is a message from B's Parent to A's Child. So far, the transaction is a Parent-Child exchange.

3. With the third message, A introduces a *switch* or *crossed transaction*, in which A berates B (a Parent-to-Child message) because "You never show any affection! You only care about yourself!" With this transaction, A gains a *payoff* of psychological superiority. Once B feels guilty for having scolded A, B accepts a *one-down status* (a Child ego state) and has lost the game.

The crossed-arrow configuration of the diagram is a characteristic of transactional games. This switch might be described as changing the subject because the gamesman always introduces a message that is conceptually different from the preceding messages. In the "Kick Me" game, for example, the subject is changed from A's desire for affection to B's selfishness. Unprepared for the switch, Person B is caught off guard.

Implicit in Berne's approach to games is an ethic: a self-actualizing person should be able to move freely along the continuum of emotional involvement with others, without relying on games as a basis for transacting. For the gamesman, the primary social function of the transactional game is to prevent intimacy. By establishing a "one-up" status with the other member of the dyad, the gamesman can create and maintain a state of psychological separation that he finds "safe."

DISCUSSION

The Transactional Games Model is a simple model that represents a great deal of real-world experience. We have used it on two basic levels of learning. First, it focuses attention on the dysfunctional strategies that many people use to protect themselves from the emotional risks of intimacy. The model is highly compatible with the Life Positions Model (OK/NOT-OK) for experimenting with new ways of thinking and behaving.

Secondly, we have applied the model to the management of the individual's own transactions with others. It is a useful conceptual framework for dealing with an inveterate gamesman. If an individual is aware that he is being enticed into a game, he has the option of maintaining an Adult ego state, analyzing the transaction, and offering the gamesman some alternatives to the reassurance of the "payoff."

Berne's descriptive names reveal the nature of each game, for example: If It Weren't For You, I'm Only Trying To Help, or Now I've Got You,

You Son-of-a-Bitch (NIGYSOB). The exploration of games will provide most participants with significant insights into the source of much of the unhappiness in their lives—becoming entrapped in game playing with the people around them.

SUGGESTED READINGS

Anderson, J. P. A transactional primer. In J. E. Jones & J. W. Pfeiffer (Eds.), *The 1973 annual handbook for group facilitators.* La Jolla, Calif.: University Associates, 1973.

Berne, E. *Games people play.* New York: Grove Press, 1964.

Harris, T. A. *I'm OK—You're OK: A practical guide to transactional analysis.* New York: Avon Books, 1973.

Convergence Strategies

The Convergence Strategies Model was developed by Walt Boshear and Karl Albrecht to deal with the concept of motion in relationships between people. It leads to deliberate strategies for establishing, maintaining, and improving relationships.

Stable, Converging, or Diverging Relationships

The model categorizes all relationships as *stable, converging,* or *diverging*. In a stable relationship, two persons have reached a conscious or unconscious agreement regarding the ways they will relate to one another. They avoid any behavior that will change the relationship. On the other hand, relationships that are in a state of change can be either converging or diverging. A converging relationship is changing in ways that enhance the benefits of the relationship to the participants. A diverging relationship is changing in ways that tend to destroy the relationship or detract from its benefits to the participants.

Personal vs. Impersonal Relationships

Any of the three types of relationships can be predominantly *personal* or predominantly *impersonal*. At the personal extreme, the ego-involvement of the participants—their attitudes, beliefs, and feelings—are an integral part of the relationship. On the other hand, emotional and personal issues are not considered in the impersonal relationship and generally will be disruptive to it if they arise.

A premise of the model is that forces, such as the consequences of growing up and the mores of Western culture, push individuals in the direction of *impersonal, stable* relationships. From birth through adolescence, the individual is cast in a role of dependency and inadequacy. He is surrounded by people who, by virtue of their age and experience, are better able to cope with their environment and who have been placed in a position of authority over him by cultural tradition. In Western culture, the individual is taught to control his emotions and follow the traditions of his society. He is strongly encouraged to refrain from making any emotional attachments except those that are approved by society, such as courtship, marriage, and a few close friendships.

In addition to the forces of culture that guide the individual in establishing and maintaining relationships with people, there are the forces of time and exposure. The human intellectual and emotional system is highly adaptive and it tends toward stability. Experiences that initially may provoke a strong intellectual or emotional response will, when sustained or repeated, tend to elicit a lesser response.

Figure 19 diagrams the structure of the model and the relationships between its elements. The internal arrows indicate the natural course of relationships under the influence of time, exposure, and cultural force. A relationship that originates with or presently has the characteristics described in any of the squares in the diagram tends to progress in the direction shown by the arrows. However, this progress is contingent upon the absence of deliberate strategies by the participants or disruptive events outside the relationship.

Stable relationships tend to remain stable, but will, through time, incline toward repetitive behaviors and coexistence of the participants. Probably the most typical example is the course of many courtships and marriages. Initially a man and woman develop a highly personal, caring relationship. As they spend more time together, the relationship is converging and the personal stake that each feels in the relationship increases. At the point of marriage and during the early honeymoon phase, they are at the peak of a high-intensity, interdependent phase. As time goes by and each becomes more familiar with the other, the relationship stabilizes as a warm, personal marriage of sharing and cooperation. If the marriage partners are not innovative in keeping their relationship on a personal basis, it gradually becomes more and more impersonal until, in many cases, they can be said only to be sharing the same residence. They reach a highly repetitive, impersonal, coexistent phase that may go on indefinitely unless it is disrupted and results in competition, withdrawal or combat. Then the relationship tends to restabilize at the same or lower level of personal commitment or deteriorate through competition or withdrawal.

If the individuals in a relationship *want to* increase their personal involvement, then they must learn and apply deliberate strategies to cause converging to happen and to maintain the new relationship state. Suggested by the model, the following are some applicable strategies.

Awareness of process. Individuals who are involved in a relationship should be *aware of the process* of that relationship. This requires them to learn about relationships in general and acquire a conceptual framework and vocabulary for monitoring the progress of their own relationship.

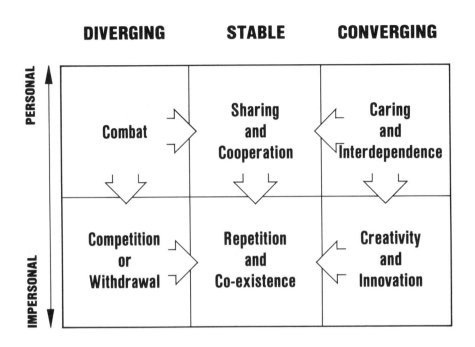

Figure 19. The impact of cultural forces on relationships

Allocation of time. Whether or not the relationship involves a *task* (problem, sport, or hobby, etc.), at least some time should be devoted to *maintaining* the relationship and meeting the *individual* needs of the participants. Although those needs may not directly be a part of the relationship, they must be dealt with in order for the individuals to continue in the relationship.

Communication skills. On one hand, verbal language provides more opportunities for misunderstanding than for understanding, and on the other hand, many things that are vitally important to a relationship cannot be verbalized at all. Consequently, people should develop their skills in both *verbal* and *nonverbal* communication about a wide range of subjects that may be relevant to the relationship, such as emotions, feelings, thoughts, ideas, beliefs, suspicions, fears, and apprehensions.

Options for behaving and feeling. Any extended relationship between people places numerous demands on their behavior and feelings. In order to respond to these situations in ways that are appropriate and beneficial to the relationship, the participants need to develop a range of *options* for behavior and feelings. For example, person A establishes a normal pattern of being understanding whenever person B takes advantage of their friendship. Repetition of that behavior can establish such strong reinforcement that A may feel he has lost the option to become angry about it. The reverse may also be true: an established pattern of anger may lead to the loss of the option to be understanding.

Willingness to risk. Disturbing a "safe" and "satisfactory" relationship can lead to improving the benefits of the relationship for the participants, but it requires their willingness to take *emotional risks*. They must be willing and able to trust each other and to expose themselves to anger, fear, joy, and even rejection as a "down payment" on deeper understanding and more rewarding relationships.

DISCUSSION

The Convergence Strategies Model can lead into structured or nonstructured experiences that enable group participants to learn and practice the skills and strategies for counteracting the forces of time, exposure, and culture. Many examples may be found in a group to demonstrate the inferences and operation of the model. Presented early in the session, the model can serve as a frequent reference point to evoke an understanding of the ongoing processes and the reason for learning such skills.

Because the model focuses directly on the cultural forces that will act on individuals as they leave the "isolation" of the learning environment, it can be used to prime group members for the re-entry process. It provides a conceptual framework for examining the probable consequences of these cultural forces and the options that are available to counteract them.

The model is particularly well suited to the interests and needs of people who are associated in long-term dyadic relationships, such as married couples and other family members. They can use it to visualize and verbalize their problems—making them easier to deal with.

There is a minor problem with the model—it is slightly more complex than many, requiring longer to develop and explore with a group. Frequently, clarifying the concepts and exploring relevant examples lengthen the presentation and discussion. This extended focus *on the model* can distract a growth or encounter group from a "here-and-now" orientation.

SUGGESTED READINGS

Bandura, W., & Walters, R. *Social learning and personality development.* New York: Holt, Rinehart and Winston, 1963.

Davis, J. H. *Group performance.* Reading, Mass.: Addison-Wesley, 1969.

Festinger, L., Riecken, H. W., Jr., & Schachter, S. *When prophecy fails.* Minneapolis, Minn.: University of Minnesota Press, 1956.

O'Neill, N., & O'Neill, G. *Open marriage: A new life style for couples.* New York: M. Evans, 1972.

Simmel, E. C., Hoppe, R. A., & Milton, G. A. (Eds.). *Social facilitation and initiative behavior.* Boston: Allyn & Bacon, 1968.

CONCLUSION TO
DYAD MODELS

Most of the really important interactions in life are between two persons. This fact has nurtured the development of significant and diverse dyad models. Some models have a very narrow band of application—they clarify or explain a specific transaction between two people. Others are more comprehensive—they construct a framework within which all types of transactions are encompassed.

In our experience, the more comprehensive a model tries to be, the more removed it is from the immediate needs of people in a learning situation. They may find the model interesting or even enlightening, but it does not provide specific answers to the issues they are wrestling with.

We selected the two-person models for this section because they facilitate what we call the "Aha!" process. Sometimes when two people are in the throes of an absorbing situation—be it conflict or joy—they reach a point of confusion and do not know where to turn. With dyad models we can help them to *realize* (to make real) the nature of their difficulties. Almost immediately they can see some specific solutions to their problem and begin to work it out.

When two people are interacting with one another, a third factor is introduced—the *relationship* itself. This must be accounted for in the model. It is useful to consider the establishment and maintenance of the relationship as a process that modifies, and, in some cases, completely subverts individual processes. If a relationship gives the parties partial or complete satisfaction of their individual needs, then they must apply some of their individual efforts and resources to the maintenance and growth of the relationship itself.

PART 3
GROUP MODELS

INTRODUCTION TO
GROUP MODELS

For many years behavioral scientists have recognized that a group has a behavior apart from the individual or dyadic processes occurring within the group. It is apparent that an individual behaves differently within a group than he does when he is alone or with another person. The models in this section describe this group-related behavior.

As can be expected, the diversity of types and sizes of groups provides a rich source for the development of models. More complex but less specific than individual or dyad models, group models are constructed at a higher level of abstraction. Groups themselves are abstractions; they do not "exist" in the same sense that an individual or a dyad exists. A group exists only as a perception of the individuals who are involved either as members or as observers.

In talking about and studying groups, an awareness of the tenuous nature of the "thing" being analyzed can save a great deal of wasted speculation. We find it helpful to return repeatedly to the level of the individual and his interactions with others. An individual does not interact with a *group*, but with other *individuals* whose behavior is influenced by the presence of others and by their perceptions of their relationships within the group.

For most people, the group they *experience* is in fact a very specific set of people with whom they have interpersonal relations. It may constitute one particular region of a larger group that is perceived more abstractly and with less immediacy. The local group cannot be completely isolated from the larger group because they share an overlapping membership. For example, the secretaries within some business organizations constitute a recognizable group; that is, they perceive themselves as belonging to a social element with distinct membership requirements. The executives of a company sometimes speak of themselves as "we" and their employees as "they." These examples suggest that a definition of a group is *perceptual*. An individual perceives a collection of people and processes as a group, and if he feels himself somehow included within that framework, then he "belongs."

Degrees of Member Influence

Some very important characteristics of groups are difficult to model, such as the degree of member influence. Figure A suggests a classification of groups according to their degree of *determinism*. At one extreme, a group with a high degree of individual influence may be called *nondeterministic*, or *stochastic*. It has the following characteristics:

- The objectives, functions, and activities of the group are established by the members—individually or collectively.

- The structure of the group and the roles of the members are dynamic and change in response to the needs and desires of the group members.

- The membership is voluntary in the sense that members are not subject to strong economic or external social pressures to maintain membership. Individuals remain members only as long as they reap some personal benefit from the association.

At another extreme is the group with a low degree of member influence. This deterministic type of group, frequently found in business and other highly structured organizations, has the following characteristics:

- The objectives and activities of the group are established outside the group, or by a few select members, or by tradition or convention. The majority of individual members see the group's objectives and activities as *given*—something they cannot readily change.

- The group's structure and roles are well defined and relatively static. The authority, relationships, and roles of the individual members are perpetuated, although different members move in and out of the group's structural "slots."

- External social or economic pressures serve to enforce and perpetuate membership beyond the point where the individual member is benefiting from the association and despite the fact that continued membership may be destructive to the individual's objectives.

Group Size

A second important characteristic of groups is size. In practice, there seems to be a natural upper limit to group size that seldom exceeds twenty persons, except for very short durations. Increasing the size of the group

	DETERMINISTIC	QUASI-DETERMINISTIC	NON-DETERMINISTIC
MEMBERSHIP	Formal Elective or appointed	Group-established criteria	Voluntary
STRUCTURE	Formal Relatively unchanging Multilevel	Sufficient to assure task performance	Subject to interpersonal dynamics
LEADERSHIP	Formal Well-established prerogatives	Consciously elected or selected	Emergent
TASKS	Clearly established, included and excluded activities	Decided by consensus within general framework	Indeterminate Subject to frequent change
LONGEVITY	Pre-established permanent or ad hoc	Determined by task features	Indeterminate Determined by individual rewards

Figure A. Group characteristics as a function of member influence.

beyond this limitation inevitably results in a formal or informal subgrouping. When this occurs, the usefulness of group models for understanding the total group is diminished, and it is more effective to consider each of the subgroups as a group.

The upper limit to group size is not entirely a function of the number of people, but is a complex relationship of several factors. As the size of a group increases, the number of *possible* interactions between the members increases geometrically. However, it is apparent from the observation of groups that there is also a limit to the number of interpersonal relationships that any individual can or wants to maintain. It is when the number of possible interactions exceeds this limit that the inevitable subgrouping takes place.

There is no reliable way to predict what will happen to the total group when subgrouping takes place. The group may dissolve, with each subgroup going its own way, or it may be sustained in many other forms, both formal and informal. In most groups, some sort of leadership function will evolve. It may be dynamic, moving from member to member, or it may remain relatively static in one member. Whether earned or formal, the nature of the leader's authority can profoundly affect the functions of the group.

The division of the group into leader/member subsets creates a hierarchy. When the second level of hierarchy is created, a new role emerges for at least one member, requiring him to be a member of two interfacing subsets of people. In the superordinate subset he has a dependent role, and in the subordinate subset he has an authority or leadership role.

An example of the emergence of these different roles and relationships can be seen in a group of people who meet to discuss a new property tax to be levied in their community. Initially they may just meet together and discuss the issue. However, if they decide to take some action, they probably will elect a chairman to lead the group—establishing one level of hierarchy. Because they have assigned him a certain authority to decide and direct their behavior, the personality of the new chairman will have more influence on the group members than that of any other member. As the group grows larger and members become engaged in many different activities, they probably will form subcommittees. Each of the subcommittee chairmen is a leader to his subcommittee and his personality will heavily influence the members. At the same time, however, the subcommittee chairmen form a group under the influence of the overall chairmen, making a second-level hierarchy.

The group models in this section may be very applicable to the behavior and dynamics of each of the subcommittees, but they will be less effective in explaining the dynamics of the total group. We have selected these models because they provide a basic foundation in group behavior;

they are conceptually simple and seem broadly applicable in facilitating learning. Some have been modified to make them serve our purposes better. We have tried to present a balanced treatment of the major areas in which readers are likely to be interested.

The study of groups is in its infancy. Only in recent years have students of human behavior begun to fully realize the impact of groups on individual behavior and attempted to model them separately. It is only natural, therefore, that group models will be less well developed than those in other categories. In some cases, group models have reached only the stage of gathering and classifying what appears to be relevant information. The maturity of the models must await further study and understanding of the immense complexities of group processes.

 **Group Structure and Process**

The Group Structure and Process Model identifies major internal relationships that exist within all groups. The ideas encompassed by the model were originated by Eric Berne in his studies on the dynamics of groups. A simplified representation of these concepts is shown in Figure 20.

Berne identifies a *group space* that relates both to the *physical* space identified as "belonging" to the group while it is in session and to the abstract, *psychological* space described as the "identity" of the group. The group identifies, at least subjectively, its own boundaries in both the physical and psychological senses. In a physical sense, the group space might represent a conference room, a house, a club, or another area that is distinguished as belonging to the group, either temporarily or permanently. In the psychological sense, the boundary is not as distinct, but an *external boundary* is drawn roughly between group members and non-group members. Everything outside the group space is indiscriminately labeled as the *external environment*.

Within the group space, Berne defines a *major internal boundary* separating the *members* from the *leadership*. This boundary may or may not be represented by the physical arrangement of the group members when they are in session, but it exists conceptually at all times. The *membership region* itself is divided by the physical and conceptual distinctions between the individual members. These are called *minor internal boundaries*.

Within this conceptual framework, Berne identifies three group forces (represented in Figure 20) that may place demands on the resources of the group:

The major group process represents interactions between members (one or more) and the leadership—these may be in the form of support or of challenge of the leadership. Frequently, both kinds of interaction will be operative at the same time because some members support while others challenge the credibility, authority, action, or some other characteristics of the leadership.

The minor group process describes interactions between group members. "Minor" refers to the importance of these interactions to the group—they may not be minor to the individuals concerned. These

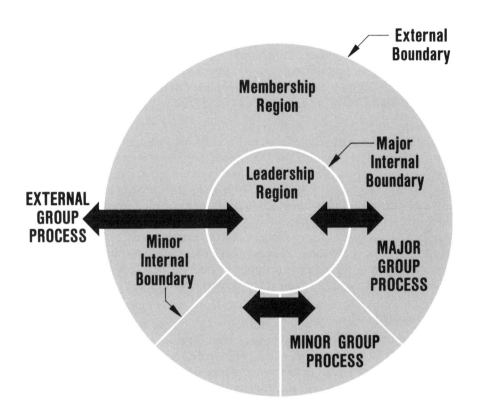

Figure 20. Group structure and process
(Adapted from Berne 1963)

minor internal processes include all the interactions occurring between members as they establish and maintain the satisfactory relationships that allow the group to continue its existence.

The external group process identifies the areas in which the group as a whole interacts with the external environment. These external processes may be routine or emergency, active or reactive. For example, a work group may give a routine progress report to an external person, or an ongoing group may suddenly be confronted with an intrusion from an external force.

Berne hypothesized that *group cohesion* is a force that operates to maintain the orderly existence of any group. He stated that the measure of group cohesion is the ability of the group to do work against opposition, i.e., to overcome external pressure and internal agitation.

The definitions of the leadership region and the membership region do not imply that these regions are necessarily identified with specific individuals. The model may be compared to a snapshot of the group—it applies to the leader and members at a particular point in time. Nor does the model imply that the leadership region is occupied by only a single person—it may represent a number of people. In a family situation, for example, the leadership region may be occupied by both parents.

DISCUSSION

Like many of Berne's models, the Group Structure and Process Model is exceptional because it represents a high order of abstraction, and yet it has many direct applications to everyday problems.

On a number of occasions, this model has been effective in clearing up some problems of business groups. It focuses attention on how the effectiveness of work groups can be eroded by infighting and interorganizational competition. Group participants may be asked to list specific examples of their activities in each of the group-process areas for a week or a month, estimating the percentage of time they devote to each activity. Subsequently, they gather in subgroups or dyads to explore alternatives to any undesirable results that have come to light.

Sometimes when two members of an encounter group are at odds, they try to use the major-group process to solve a problem best approached with the techniques of the minor-group process. This misuse of the group can be exposed by the model, resulting in a more productive one-to-one process for the group participants.

SUGGESTED READING

Berne, E. *The structure and dynamics of organizations and groups.* New York: Grove Press, 1963.

 **Communication Networks**

A number of researchers have examined specific interpersonal relationships within a group and diagrammed them as networks of communication between members. This model presents some of these communication networks as they affect the social structure and performance of a group.

Communication networks are easily diagrammed in groups of three, four, and five persons, as shown in Figure 21.1. However, interactions in larger groups become very complex and cannot readily be illustrated by the network technique. In the network imagery, the small circles represent people in the group and the connecting lines represent their interpersonal channels of communication and interaction.

When relationships are *imposed* on a group, they are commonly referred to as *formal* networks. When the networks *emerge* as a result of the desires and preferences of group members, they are considered *informal*. Informal networks coexist in a group where formal networks have been imposed. In groups that employ paper as a formal means of communication (letters, memos, etc.), the informal network may operate much faster and more efficiently than the formal network—sometimes rendering the formal network virtually useless except for historical "documentation."

The networks in Figure 21.1 are arranged in increasing order of the number of relationship channels available. Studies have shown that the efficiency of a group does not increase linearly with an increase of channels.

Because a relationship is different for each person in that relationship, *direction* of the information flow or the attraction between individuals can be added to the network diagrams. Some individuals are strongly attracted to others who hardly notice them. Figure 21.2 illustrates how this concept of direction can be applied to the simple three-person diagram to create additional network possibilities.

Another important consideration in communication networks is the relationship of certain people to the environment external to the group. This can have a tremendous impact on the way information flows between the group members and the "outside world." It is quite common in groups that only certain members are authorized to interact with people outside the group. Figures 21.3 to 21.5 show three possible configurations for a group of three people and three relationships to *group space* and an *environment*. In Figure 21.3, members B and C of the triad will know only what member A tells them about the external environment. In 21.4, members B and C will have information from outside the group, but member A will not. In 21.5, all three members receive and share their observations about the external environment.

DISCUSSION

Analyzing the relationships in a group as communication networks can provide the facilitator with much valuable data for diagnosing group processes. Although defining the group structure in terms of communication networks is subjective, it can be quite revealing. In organizations, many cases of poor performance by employees can be traced to an individual's location in a group network diagram—he may lack vital information required for a good performance.

As a way of understanding and coping with internal problems, the facilitator may wish to have a group construct a network diagram representing its own structure. The group could also develop and implement a more functional network for meeting its objectives.

In groups of more than five people, the network form of presenting the data can become very complex. As an alternate technique, the facilitator can construct a *sociomatrix*, as illustrated in Figure 21.6. This sociomatrix corresponds to the network diagrammed in Figure 21.4 and is quite simple. Individuals are represented by A, B, and C. The rows in the diagram represent the *initiator* of the communication (output). The columns represent the *receiver* (input). At each intersection, a blank cell indicates *no connection* and an X represents a *connection*. In this example, the fourth row and column represent the *environment*; B and C receive input from the environment, but they do not initiate any output. By examining the rows, it can be seen that everyone initiates communication to someone. However, the columns show that A receives no information from anywhere and is the isolated member of the group.

In experiential learning environments, the Communication Networks Model is useful as a tool for group development. For example, the facilitator can lead the group in developing a diagram of preferences. The arrows of the diagram could represent a preference for affiliation with one person above others. Each person privately chooses one person he prefers above others for some association, e.g., having lunch, playing cards, talking, etc. When shared and diagrammed, the choices become a tool that can be used by the group for self-examination and discussion.

SUGGESTED READINGS

Bavelas, A. Communication patterns in task-oriented groups. *Journal of the Acoustical Society of America*, 1950, *22*, 725-730.

Bavelas, A., & Barrett, D. An experimental approach to organizational communication. *Personnel*, 1951, *27*, 367-371.

Davis, J. H. *Group performance*. Reading, Mass.: Addison-Wesley, 1969.

Leavitt, H. J. Some effects of certain patterns on group performance. *Journal of Abnormal and Social Psychology*, 1951, *46*, 367-371.

Figures 21.1 through 21.6 are on the following pages.

THREE-PERSON NETWORKS

FOUR-PERSON NETWORKS

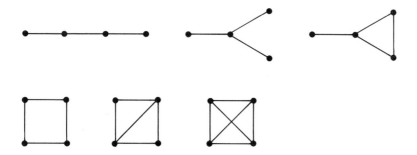

FIVE-PERSON NETWORKS

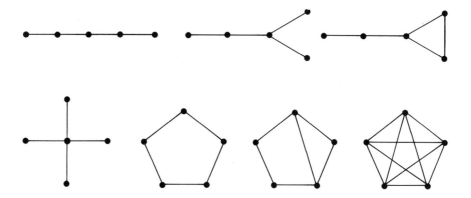

Figure 21.1.   Some possible communications networks in small groups

(Adapted from *Group Performance* by James H. Davis, Addison-Wesley, Reading, Mass., 1969. Used with permission of the publisher.)

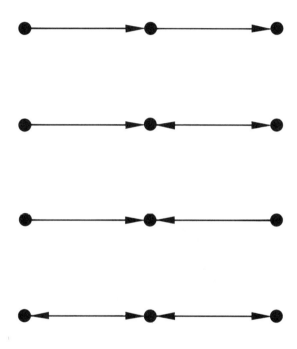

Figure 21.2. The "direction" of information flow in communications networks

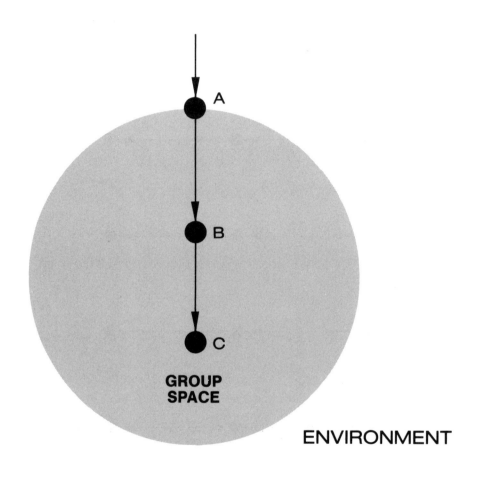

Figure 21.3. The isolated group

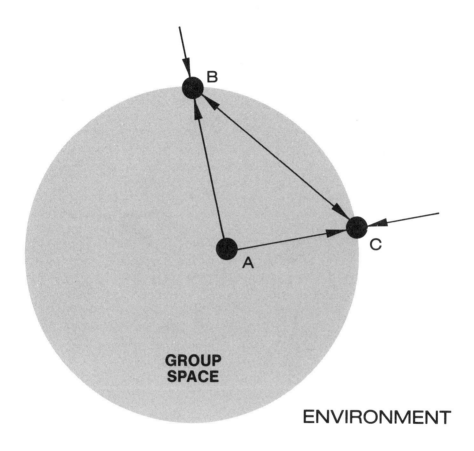

GROUP
SPACE

ENVIRONMENT

Figure 21.4.   The isolated group member

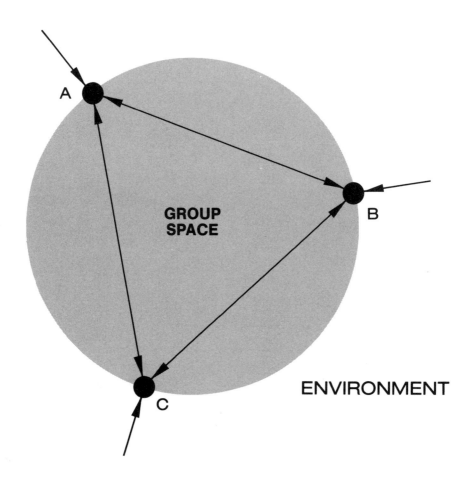

Figure 21.5. Full information flow in a small group

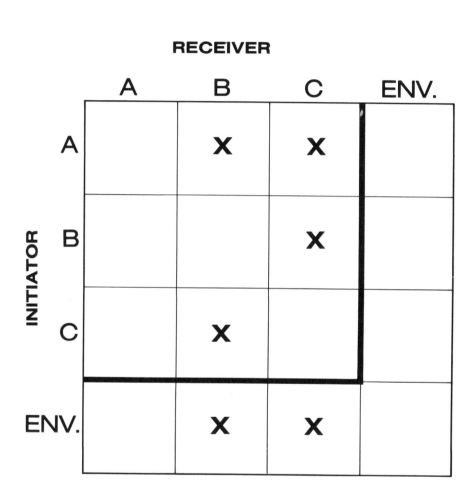

Figure 21.6. Sociomatrix of Figure 21.4

Behaviorial Influences of Groups

When a person becomes a member of a group, certain forces come into play to influence his behavior. These forces exist because of his membership in the group and do not operate on nongroup members. Some of these behavioral influences and their implications are described in this model and diagrammed in Figure 22. Walt Boshear based the model on many research observations of group process.

Membership

Each person in a group feels a specific degree of *membership* in that group. The strength of this feeling depends on the extent to which the member accepts the group's objectives and activities and finds them in common with his own personal preferences. It is also related to the measure of acceptance he feels from the other group members. An individual member behaves differently toward group members than toward nonmembers and his behavior is influenced by the degree of membership he feels. Strong membership feelings result in supportive behavior toward other members and protective behavior against nonmembers.

Role

Each member of a group assumes a *role* or is assigned a role by other members. This role may be considered a set of expectations regarding the way the individual will behave in the group. He may have the role of expert, leader, follower, observer, recorder, disrupter, organizer, etc. The individual's behavior tends to be consistent with his perception of the role he is expected or expects to play in the group.

Authority

Group members usually behave in accordance with imposed or accepted *authority* relationships—authority assigned or assumed by individuals. In some groups, these authority relationships are formally defined, in others they emerge as a result of individual expertise or influence. Once these authority relationships are established, group members tend to behave in accordance with the dictates of the authority figures.

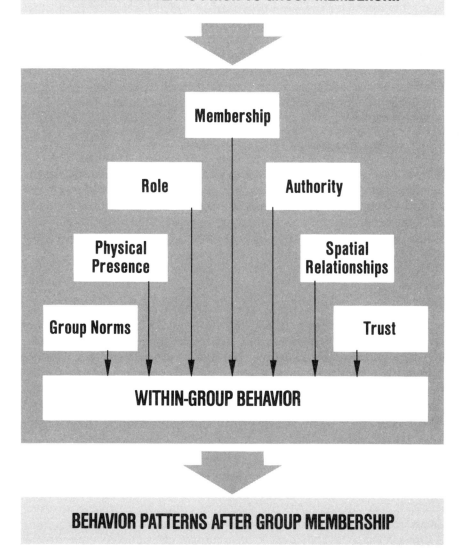

Figure 22. Behavioral influence of groups

Physical Presence

Group members are heavily influenced by the *physical presence* of other members. The presence or absence of individual members may directly affect the role, authority, degree of participation, or influence of other members. Low participators may become high participators in a group session when only one member is absent. The physical absence of one member may cause a dramatic change in authority, roles, and other established relationships, although the absent individual is still a member of the group.

Spatial Relationships

The physical *arrangement* of the group and the physical *proximity* of the members will influence their behavior. For example, individuals at the head of a table tend to be assigned more authority than others. Standing members tend to command more attention than seated members. Individuals who are in close proximity tend to influence one another's behavior more than individuals who are separated by more distance.

Norms

Each group evolves behavioral *norms* that strongly influence individual behavior. These norms establish the propriety of certain types of behavior, identifying behavioral and subject taboos that group members would be punished for violating. The group norm determines whether feelings are a legitimate subject for group consideration, whether jokes are appropriate, or whether members are allowed to move around the room or must sit still. Individuals become sensitive to these norms and usually behave in ways that are consistent with them.

Trust

A high priority for each group member is the protection of his feelings and attitudes—his ego. The degree to which an individual trusts other members of the group regulates the degree to which he is willing to reveal himself to them. If he lacks trust in other members, he will not reveal more of himself than he considers safe, shutting off valuable input to the group's knowledge or process. An individual determines his degree of trust by observing how other members reveal themselves and then subjectively evaluating the result, such as the consistency between verbal and nonverbal messages from the other members.

Within-Group Behavior

The model implies that *within-group behavior* will influence the individual's behavior outside the group, although that outside behavior probably will be different from his behavior inside the group. Essentially, the degree to which the individual's behavior outside the group is influenced depends on his personal involvement in the group and the usefulness of within-group behaviors to him.

DISCUSSION

We find this model very effective for communicating to groups the distinction between the group process and the rest of the world. It helps to make the point that there is no reason why an individual's behavior in the group must be consistent with his behavior outside the group. When used in experiential groups as a part of the early establishment of group norms, the model helps members realize that they have an option both for experimentation within the group and for changing external behaviors.

Many people who enter an encounter group are afraid of experimenting with new behaviors because they feel they might lose their former behavioral options. This model allays some of those fears by focusing attention on the individual's right to modify his behavior.

On several occasions, we have used the Behavioral Influences of Groups Model as an introduction to a discussion about re-entry into the outside world. It sets the stage for examining the in-group behaviors that have evolved during the group session and for developing strategies for coping with the external environment.

SUGGESTED READINGS

Argyle, M. *The psychology of interpersonal behavior.* Baltimore, Md.: Penguin Books, 1967.

Cartwright, D., & Zander, A. *Group dynamics: Research and theory.* New York: Harper & Row, 1968.

Hanson, P. G. What to look for in groups: An observation guide. In J. W. Pfeiffer & J. E. Jones (Eds.), *The 1972 annual handbook for group facilitators.* La Jolla, Calif.: University Associates, 1972.

Heslin, R. Predicting group task effectiveness from member characteristics. *Psychological Bulletin*, 1964, 4, 248-256.

Jackson, J. Structural characteristics of norms. In I. D. Steiner & M. Fishbein (Eds.), *Current studies in social psychology.* New York: Holt, Rinehart and Winston, 1965.

A·E·I·O·U

The A-E-I-O-U Model, developed by Karl Albrecht, categorizes certain key roles and relationships within groups that are formal but loosely structured. The letters A-E-I-O-U stand for five functional roles:

Action Person. A doer, the Action Person hungers for results and has little patience with procrastination, deliberation, or philosophizing. Show him a goal and he is first in line to try to reach it.

Energizer. Capable of motivating others, the Energizer inspires them to tap their potentials for the common objective. He can recognize valuable ideas, set objectives, and help others to see that the goals are attainable.

Idea Person. After quietly studying a problem, the Idea Person can come up with an exciting new approach to solving it. He produces masses of new concepts, new techniques, and new possibilities, but he also often generates ideas that he has not thought through. Consequently, other people do not always recognize his ideas as significant. He is happiest when deeply involved in some challenging problem.

Organizer. The Organizer gets a group together—ready to work. Given an objective and a measure of responsibility, he will make a plan, assign tasks, and manage operations so that the group can get results. He is oriented to people, relationships, and processes.

Uncommitted Person. Present and accounted for, but psychologically disengaged, the Uncommitted Person neither resists nor supports the group's objectives. He will do what he is asked to do, usually competently but without extra effort. He may be preoccupied with other ideas or activities.

Role Relationships

Very few people fall into one single A-E-I-O-U category. In a given situation, however, most people have a predominant orientation to one particular role. And pairs of individuals with different role orientations are likely to have certain modes of interaction. The relationship between the Energizer and the Action Person serves as a useful example. The Energizer probably will supply the sense of impetus—the goal or objective to be met. In fulfilling his master plan, he may enlist the efforts of the Action Person. The Action Person supplies the enthusiasm and practical competence to do the job. The Energizer seeks the Action Person's willingness to exert himself. The Action Person seeks worthwhile goals from the Energizer. Because each seeks something in the other, these two roles form a compatible pair.

Other combinations may be analyzed in a similar way, as shown in Figure 23. The combinations along the diagonal (top left to lower right) represent the behavior of an individual who is unable to form appropriate role relationships with others or who is obliged to interact solely with others of his own type. For example, an Action Person, alone or with other active persons, is likely to resort to activity for its own sake. His slogan might be "Let's do something, even if it's wrong!" To the extent that he can shift to other roles as circumstances demand it, he may be able to derive worthwhile objectives and establish needed organizational structure among his coworkers. But if he is firmly situated in his role, he probably is much less effective than he could be if he operated with people who represent compatible roles.

DISCUSSION

The A-E-I-O-U Model has many implications for analyzing social patterns and relationships within an organization. It applies particularly well to an established, conventionally functioning group, such as a department or a project team within a business organization. One way to evaluate the effectiveness of the organization is to examine the strength of its various role relationships. That is, the organization is likely to be more effective if the compatible role players have found one another, than if they have not. Moreover, an obvious deduction from the model is that an appropriate mixture of roles is desirable. For example, a group composed of many Energizers, no Idea People, a few Organizers, few Action People, and numerous Uncommitted People could not be expected to be as effective as one composed of a few Energizers and Idea People, a large number of Organizers and Action People, and few Uncommitted People.

When the four principal role players establish compatible relationships and have a certain social integrity and survival capability, they form what might be termed a "human molecule" because of the self-reinforcing quality of the composite pattern of relationships. In addition, they probably can create an atmosphere of accomplishment that encourages Uncommitted People to return to more highly involved role orientations.

DEALS WITH THIS PERSON BY:

	ACTION PERSON	ENERGIZER	IDEA PERSON	ORGANIZER	UNCOM-MITTED
ACTION PERSON	Activity for its own sake	Seeks impetus & direction	Impatience Seeks ideas that can be implemented	Accommodation May resent controls	Disregards Considers him dead wood
ENERGIZER	Motivating Inspiring Setting goals	Much talk Little action	Encouragement Nurturing new ideas	Sets objectives Gives guidance & encouragement	Arousal Motivates & stirs to an involved role
IDEA PERSON	Trying to sell ideas	Seeks encouragement validation & direction Sells ideas	Has ideas but no sense of direction or action	Tries to sell ideas Often does not succeed	Ignores
ORGANIZER	Channels & directs activities Coordinates Communicates	Seeks support and guidance	Consultation Demands solutions	Preoccupation with organization & procedures	Persuasion Coercion Direction
UNCOMMITTED	Resentment Jealousy	Complaints Rationalizations	Scorn	Passive resistance Grudging acceptance	Drifting

(Left vertical axis label: **THIS PERSON**)

Figure 23. The A-E-I-O-U model

126

Several cautions are in order concerning this model. First, the user should remind himself that many other factors come into play in organizational dynamics. The model, while quite useful, should not be used in isolation to assess an organization or to redesign it. It should serve as one input to a comprehensive process of analysis.

Secondly, the role orientations of the people within groups or organizations are not usually so well defined or so isolated as the diagram implies. In a typical organization, each individual is likely to negotiate a role that is appropriate to his relative authority (formal and informal), his social status, his functional position in the organization, and a number of other factors. A flexible individual is likely to assume a role that gives him maximum rewards within a particular setting. However, the model is quite effective for dealing with relationships among individuals who have strongly defined role orientations.

We find the A-E-I-O-U Model useful as a communication tool in organization development work. It helps to clarify relationships and the many possibilities within an organization, and it calls attention to the human side of enterprise. The model generates thoughtful discussion of the potential of human system engineering in making organizations more effective. It also provides an excellent conceptual basis for later exploration in an experiential, interpersonal atmosphere, such as a team-building session or a problem-solving workshop.

 **Group Functions**

The Group Functions Model organizes information about the nature of functions that consume a group's time and energy resources: *task, interaction,* and *self-orientation*. Walt Boshear and Karl Albrecht adapted this particular version of the model from the work of B. M. Bass to incorporate the concepts of *direct* and *indirect* activities as they affect the group process. In any group, the time and energies of the members may be considered to be directed toward one of three basic functions:

Task-oriented behavior is aimed at accomplishing the objectives of the group. These objectives might be work, play, manufacturing, or any other ouput of the group. Task-oriented activities could include proposing tasks or goals, requesting facts, offering information, clarifying issues, summarizing, consensus testing, or specific work, such as writing, building, skiing, walking, fishing, etc.

Interaction-oriented activities relate to the group process. They are directed at the operation of the group as a group. Behaviors that may indicate attention to the interaction-oriented function are the following: encouraging, expressing feelings, attempting to reconcile disagreements, compromising one's position for the benefit of the group, attempting to keep communication channels open, and setting or applying standards for group performance.

Self-oriented activities relate to meeting individual needs rather than helping the group in its task. These behaviors may include emphasizing personal issues, concerns, desires, and needs; dominating the discussion; interrupting others; wasting time; not listening; pouting, etc. Self-oriented activities may or may not be helpful to the task-oriented or interaction-oriented functions of the group.

Direct and Indirect Activities

The activities of the individual members in relation to the three basic functions may be *direct* or *indirect*. In direct behavior there is agreement between the apparent reason for a member's behavior and the real reason. Indirect behavior is motivated by a reason the member does not reveal to the group. Such covert reasons can be labeled *hidden agendas* because they are not on the open, shared agenda of the group. For example, if a group member supports an idea simply because he thinks it is a good one, he is engaging in direct behavior. If, however, he overtly supports the idea as a way to gain favor with the person who introduced the idea, then he has a hidden agenda and is engaging in indirect behavior. Figure 24 graphically shows the relationship of the model's concepts and the range of possibilities for group functioning.

Each group has its own characteristic way of performing the three basic functions. In a "closed" group the primary *direct* activities are restricted to task-oriented functions. The members give direct attention to interaction-oriented functions only if they are necessary to the task. For example, a certain amount of social behavior is allowed as a concession to getting acquainted, provided that it does not go on too long. Personal issues or self-oriented behaviors are discouraged.

In contrast to closed groups, there are other groups with norms that are more tolerant of interaction-oriented and self-oriented behaviors. The self-orientation of the members is even the primary focus of some groups in which interaction issues are dealt with only to the extent that they do not interfere with the personal needs of the individual members. The group either has no task or is so enmeshed in personal issues that the task receives no direct attention.

DISCUSSION

This model provides a vocabulary and conceptual framework that is effective for a group's discussion of establishing and maintaining its norms and planning its expenditure of resources.

The model can also be used to facilitate a group's ability to observe and monitor its own group processes. Small discussion groups can be formed, each with an observer. The observer records for subsequent processing the behaviors he categorizes as task-oriented, interaction-oriented, and self-oriented.

SUGGESTED READINGS

Bass, B. M. *Manual for orientation inventory.* Palo Alto, Calif.: Consulting Psychologists Press, 1962.

Lippitt, G. L. & Seashore, E. W. *The leader looks at group effectiveness.* Washington, D. C.: Leadership Resources, 1961.

INDIVIDUAL BEHAVIOR

INDIRECT ◄─────────────────────────► DIRECT

GROUP FUNCTION		INDIRECT	DIRECT
	TASK	Subtle attempts to push personal projects or to sabotage group efforts	Open participation in the work, play, etc., activities of the group
	INTERACTION	Hidden agreements with other group members Suppression or avoidance of interpersonal issues	Open confrontation of interpersonal issues
	SELF	Personal desires, needs, and objectives kept private Disruptive attempts to get attention	Open disclosure of personal needs, desires, etc., for group attention

Figure 24. Direct and indirect individual behavior in group functions

25 Hill Interaction Matrix (HIM)

The HIM Model emerged as William Fawcett Hill was developing an instrument for measuring group interaction styles. It is a comprehensive method for thinking about and discussing group characteristics. The model describes and categorizes group interactions from two perspectives, *content* and *work style*.

Content

In classifying the subjects of group interactions, Hill identified four typical categories: *topics, group, personal,* and *relationship*. The first two content categories are oriented toward nonmembers, and the latter two are oriented toward members. The Topics category refers to subjects of general interest that are external to the group or the members. The Group content includes interactions that have the group and the group processes as subjects. An interaction with one of the members as the subject would be categorized as Personal content. The Relationship category covers the subject of interactions between group members.

Work Style

The work style of a group is divided into four categories: *conventional, assertive, speculative,* and *confrontive*. Hill considers Conventional and Assertive to be *pre-work* styles, while Speculative and Confrontive represent the *work* proper. Figure 25 illustrates the two dimensions of group interaction—content and work style—in matrix form. The work style dimension will be used to discuss the nature of the intersections.

Conventional. In the conventional mode, the group members hold fast to patterned and socially acceptable behaviors. Topical discussions are general, concerning subjects about which most members can agree or, at least, be objective. When the group is the subject, conversation may include operational information, such as meeting times and places, or social discussions about the group and its activities. If the members become personal, their talk is restricted to hobbies, likes, dislikes, general history, etc. The relationships discussed are very superficial, supportive, and flattering to the individuals.

| | CONTENT | | | |
| | NONMEMBER-ORIENTED | | MEMBER-ORIENTED | |
WORK STYLE	TOPICS	GROUP	PERSONAL	RELATIONSHIP
CONVENTIONAL	General	Operations Activities	Hobbies Opinions	Flattering Supportive
ASSERTIVE	Gripes	Critical attack	Show-off Bragging	Exaggerated
SPECULATIVE	Theories	Constructive evaluation	Causation Consequences	Impact analysis
CONFRONTIVE	Meaning Relevance	Processes	Underlying issues	Reality testing

PRE-WORK / WORK

Figure 25. Hill Interaction Matrix (HIM) (Adapted with permission from W. F. Hill)

Assertive. The assertive style is a pseudoconfrontation style. Although the group members may challenge each other, they do not do so for the purpose of seeking or giving help; they are merely acting out roles. Topical conversations involve gripes about the establishment, the President, the price of food, etc. Discussion about the group is critical and nonconstructive. When group members get personal in the assertive style, they brag, show-off, complain, or otherwise attempt to set themselves apart from the other group members. Relationships are frequently acted out or discussed in an exaggerated manner, either positively or negatively.

Speculative. The speculative style characterizes the cognitive work of the group members. It involves asking and answering questions and forming hypotheses. This style represents the intellectual processing of data and experiences. Topical discussions involve subjects relevant to group issues, such as behavioral theories. The group process is evaluated from a critical but constructive position, and the group seeks methods and strategies for improvement. Personal issues of members are examined for causation, consequences, alternatives, etc. Relationships are analyzed and evaluated for their importance or impact on the individual members.

Confrontive. Confrontation involves exposing oneself to personal risk, seeking and giving help in real problem areas, and making contact with others on vital issues. Topical issues in the confrontive mode are fully explored to understand all relevant meaning for the participants. In the confrontive style, group processes that have been consciously or unconsciously avoided are examined. Personal concerns of the group members are explored in depth to separate the real underlying issues from the surface distortions. The relationships between members are the subject of reality testing—looking behind assumptions and expectations to discover actual relationship issues.

Hill defines the first two styles, Conventional and Assertive, as prework because they represent the group's avoidance or pseudoconfrontation of issues, instead of its actual engagement of the issues cognitively in the Speculative style or experientially in the Confrontive mode.

Over the duration of its existence, a group may engage in all of the work styles and range over all the content areas. If a large proportion of the group time is devoted to one style or content area, then that may be referred to as the group style.

DISCUSSION

One version of the HIM includes an additional work style called *Responsive*. It is characterized by reluctant group members whose primary interaction is to respond minimally to group leader intervention. It was not included in this discussion because it is usually not encountered in learning situations, but is observed in therapy groups, which are outside the scope of this book.

The HIM Model as presented, however, can be very beneficial to a group in evaluating and monitoring its own behavior. It portrays a wide range of behaviors as possible options for the group, allowing members to conclude or adopt strategies that are most consistent with their objectives.

Not only does the model focus on characteristic behavior for the total group, but it also lends itself to analysis of individual behavior. Group members can use the vocabulary of the model in articulating their fears, concerns, or frustrations. Even a subjective positioning of individual member behavior within the HIM framework can clarify the reasons for misunderstanding and conflict between members.

Hill states that there is a deliberate value system in the arrangement of the content and work-style categories. The categories are arranged from left to right and from top to bottom in ascending order of their contribution to growth—as Hill sees it. When this value judgment is observed by group members in the presentation of the model, it is easily dealt with, and does not seem to affect the utility of the model.

For us, the most effective use of the model has been in growth groups. The model's concepts seem to have more relevance for groups that are wrestling with personal and interpersonal issues.

SUGGESTED READINGS

Hill, W. F. Hill interaction matrix (HIM) conceptual framework for understanding groups. In J. E. Jones & J. W. Pfeiffer (Eds.), *The 1973 annual handbook for group facilitators.* La Jolla, Calif.: University Associates, 1973.

Hill, W. F. *Hill interaction matrix (HIM).* California State Polytechnic University (Pomona), 1965.

26 Group Orientations

While applying his theory of Transactional Analysis to the study of groups, Eric Berne developed this model as a simple but useful conceptual framework for discussing group orientations. Berne concluded that groups could be classified initially by the direction in which their tasks were oriented—*external* or *internal* as shown in Figure 26.

External

An externally oriented group performs tasks and activities that "engage the environment." The "work" of the group is intended in some way to be applied outside the group.

In *nonthreatening* environments, the group can be called an activity or *work* group. Such groups might be engaged in skiing, camping, farming, studying, training, manufacturing, selling, or performing. These activities primarily are aimed at working to change the environment or enjoying it.

In a *threatening* environment, the externally oriented group might be referred to as a *combat* group. It engages the environment for the *protection* and survival of the group structure or the individual interests that the group members hold in common. Social-activist groups, community-action groups, and strikers are typical groups of this type.

Internal

Internally oriented groups are concerned with the processes within the group itself: structure, relationships, agitations, etc. The environment may be either threatening or nonthreatening. This type of group Berne called a *process group*.

Expenditure of Resources

In classifying groups, Berne was concerned with the *expenditure of resources* of the group. Because the resources—time, energy, money, influence—of any group are limited, the way in which they are expended directly affects the group's achievement. For example, a group that forms as a work group and then finds itself torn by internal conflicts and

GROUP FOCUS	ENVIRONMENT	TYPE OF GROUP	GROUP OBJECTIVE
EXTERNAL	Nonthreatening	Work	Achievement
	Threatening	Combat	Survival Protection
INTERNAL	Either	Process	Improved Structure, Relationships

Figure 26. Group orientations

competition will have to apply much of its resources to managing these internal problems. In extreme cases, these internal problems can consume *all* the group's resources, reducing the work output to zero. Another example is a group that forms as a process group and then finds itself in a hostile environment—either real or perceived. If the resources of the group are expended in combat with the environment, the members may not realize the benefits they had hoped to gain from their association.

DISCUSSION

The Group Orientations Model focuses the attention of a group on its real purpose and can serve equally well in an academic or an experiential setting.

Frequently we have found that a group changes its type, even if the members do not clearly understand the group's shift in purpose. The model can provide group members with a vocabulary for discussing and clarifying their present focus as opposed to their desired focus.

Effective as a planning tool for organization development and team building, the model indicates that an OD group may have to orient itself initially as a process group. This establishes relationships and understanding between members that enable them later to use their resources more effectively on work problems.

A principal value of this model is that it helps a group to choose the way it will expend its resources, and it allows group members to monitor whether they are performing according to plan.

SUGGESTED READINGS

Berne, E. *The structure and dynamics of organizations and groups.* New York: Grove Press, 1963.

Cartwright, D., & Zander, A. (Eds.), *Group dynamics.* Evanston, Ill.: Row, Peterson, 1953.

Cartwright, D., & Zander, A. *Group dynamics: Research and theory* (3rd ed.). New York: Harper & Row, 1968.

27 Tori Model for Group Growth

TORI is an acronym for *trust, openness, realization,* and *interdependence.* The TORI Model, developed by Jack and Lorraine Gibb, describes *group growth*—the process of change toward the TORI characteristics. Gibb and Gibb based the model on the assumption that a natural product of interaction between individuals in a group is an inherent "pressure"—a movement toward trusting and being trusted, intimate communication, self-realization and self-actualization, and genuine interdependence.

Figure 27 presents a summary of the TORI characteristics as they relate to the *climate, data flow, goal formation,* and *control* functions of a group.

Climate. When a new group forms, most of the members initially relate in ways that indicate a lack of trust. They are defensive and interact with one another from their traditional role positions. During the early phase of group development, the members are evaluating one another and forming satisfactory and safe relationships. As the group grows, people engage one another on an increasingly personal basis. The trust level increases, less formality is imposed, and members become freer in expressing their feelings and enjoying intimate relationships.

Data flow. Early in the life of a group, when fear and distrust exist, people withdraw from one another to a polite, formal distance. Their communications become garbled and distorted by the strategies they have developed for personal protection. As the group develops, increased trust between individuals leads them to a more open and direct presentation of themselves. This openness is apparent in their candor, intimacy, confrontation of issues, and direct attempts to influence one another.

Goal formation. A newly formed group approaches goal formation or productivity in a persuasive-competitive mode. Members are intent on teaching, correcting, and otherwise imposing their ideas on others. As the group matures, the members confront problems and tasks as part of an initial process of learning and searching. There is increased self-determination and realization of individual potentials that can be applied to problem solving.

138

GROUP GROWTH ➡

	Movement From:	Movement To:
Climate	Distrust Defense	Trust Intimacy
Data Flow	Formality Distance	Openness Directness
Goal Formation	Persuasion Competition	Realization Self-determination
Control	Dependence Dominance	Interdependence

Figure 27. TORI model for group growth
(Adapted with permission of Jack R. Gibb)

Control. In a new group, the members exhibit patterned behaviors related to leadership and authority because their only perceived alternatives are the traditional extremes of dependence/dominance. As the group evolves, the control issues lose their importance. Leadership becomes fluid—passing from person to person—or is absent altogether. Self-sufficient members relate interdependently as individuals.

Rather than being independent, these four general categories of group characteristics are intimately interrelated and interdependent. Growth along each of the TORI paths will proceed sporadically as progress and setbacks are encountered in the other areas.

DISCUSSION

The TORI Model has two distinctly different applications: (1) as a *technique* for facilitating growth groups; and (2) as a *conceptual framework* for understanding and communicating the growth processes of groups. These applications arise from the basic premise of the model: the growth process is a *natural* process that only needs to be allowed to happen.

When the model is used as a technique with a growth group, Gibb and Gibb suggest that the facilitator become a part of the group and attempt to facilitate his own growth, moving away from the role of trainer and toward the TORI position. They do not imply that the facilitator should abandon his responsibilities and become a passive, nondirective observer. They do suggest that he be assertive, warm, open, active, expressive, and very much involved in the decisions and processes of the group—as a full person and member of the group.

The TORI Model has value, even if one does not accept the techniques that have been developed to implement it. In a more structured environment, where a different technique is used, the facilitator can use the TORI Model as a tool for setting group goals and evaluating progress. This approach may appear to be a contradiction in concepts: if the model is valid, how can the facilitator justify his adoption of a role of responsibility and authority? The answer lies in an examination of the group's objective. If the objective of the group is personal and group growth, and the facilitator has the opportunity to participate with the group *throughout* the growth process, then the TORI technique may be implied. If, however, the objective of the group is the accomplishment of a task, and the learning facilitator has a very limited amount of time with the group, then it may be more appropriate for him to spend that time in helping the group members understand a model they can use for continuing their growth after the facilitator is gone.

SUGGESTED READINGS

Gibb, J. R. Climate for trust formation. In L. P. Bradford, J. R. Gibb, & K. D. Benne (Eds.), *T-group theory and laboratory method: Innovation in re-education.* New York: John Wiley, 1964.

Gibb, J. R. TORI theory and practice. In J. W. Pfeiffer & J. E. Jones (Eds.), *The 1972 annual handbook for group facilitators.* La Jolla, Calif.: University Associates, 1972.

Gibb, J. R. & Gibb, L. M. Emergence therapy: The TORI process in an emergent group. In G. M. Garzda (Ed.), *Innovations to group psychotherapy.* Springfield, Ill.: Charles C. Thomas, 1968.

Gibb, J. R., & Gibb, L. M. Role freedom in a TORI group. In A. Burton (Ed.), *Encounter: The theory and practice of encounter groups.* San Francisco: Jossey-Bass, 1969.

Group Development

The Group Development Model, formulated by John E. Jones, describes four stages in the evolution of a group. Each of the four phases has two major dimensions: *personal relations* and *task functions*. Jones concludes that the progress along these two paths is parallel and interrelated, as shown in Figure 28.

The personal relations dimension of the model encompasses all the interrelationships that people develop and sustain in the group—their feelings, expectations, commitments, assumptions, and problems with one another. The four stages of personal relations correlate with the development of the identity and functions of a group from the personal orientations of individual members. The four stages of task functions correlate with the progress of a group in understanding and accomplishing its work. As a group moves through the personal relations and task functions stages simultaneously, the progress and setbacks in one dimension influence the behavior and progress in the other.

Stage One

In Stage One, group members are highly *dependent* in their personal relations. They rely on safe patterned behavior and look to the group leader for guidance and direction. In their task functions, the members are getting oriented to the task. Discussion centers around defining the scope of the task, how to approach it, etc.

Stage Two

As the group members attempt to *organize* for the task at Stage Two, *conflict* inevitably results in their personal relations. Individuals have to bend and mold their feelings, ideas, attitudes, and beliefs to suit the group organization. Although conflicts may or may not surface as group issues, they do exist.

Stage Three

The major task function of Stage Three is the *data flow* between group members—they share feelings and ideas, solicit and give feedback to one

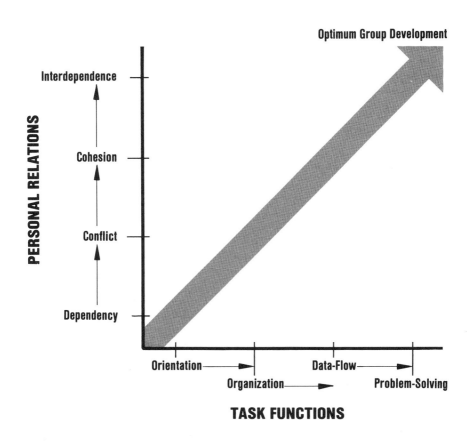

Figure 28. Model for group development
(Adapted from Jones 1974)

another, and explore actions related to the task. When members begin to know, and identify with, one another, the level of trust in their personal relations contributes to the development of group *cohesion*. If this stage of data flow and cohesion is attained by the group members, their interactions are characterized by openness and sharing of information on both a personal and task level. They feel good about being part of an effective group.

Stage Four

If group members are able to evolve to *Stage Four*, their capacity, range, and depth of personal relations expand to true *interdependence*. In this stage, people can work singly, in subgroups, or as a total unit with equal facility. Their roles and authorities dynamically adjust to the changing needs of the group and individuals. The task function becomes genuinely *problem solving*, leading toward optimal solutions and *optimum group development*.

DISCUSSION

Many have attempted to come to grips with the relationship between the human element and the productive element in groups. In the Group Development Model, Jones clarifies the process with his conceptualization of the data as parallel paths along which the group moves.

By referring to this model, a facilitator can gain some insight into the inevitable stages through which a group must pass before attaining the benefits of Stage Four. This insight is useful both in planning group learning situations and for monitoring the group's progress while it is in session.

As a communication tool, the model is most effective at Stage Three of a group's development. At this point, members have experienced Stages One and Two and are in a receptive mode to internalize the implications of State Four. The model provides them with a goal they can visualize and work toward. Paying earnest attention to strategies for reaching Stage Four can facilitate the movement to that stage.

According to our experience, if the concepts of the model are presented when a group is in Stage One, they fall on deaf ears, at most, receiving only polite attention. If presented in Stage Two, the concepts become food for conflicts or are ground into oblivion by the process of organization. And at Stage Four, the model is unnecessary.

In an academic environment, we have had difficulty in generating any useful discussion with the model. It has a very low impact and appeals only to those who enjoy taking notes.

SUGGESTED READINGS

Blake, R. R., & Mouton, J. S. *The managerial grid*. Houston, Tex.: Gulf Publishing, 1964.

Blake, R. R., & Mouton, J. S. An overview of the grid. In W. R. Lassey & R. R. Fernández (Eds.), *Leadership and social change* (2nd ed., rev.). La Jolla, Calif.: University Associates, 1976.

Hill, W. F. *Hill interaction matrix (HIM)*. California State Polytechnic University (Pomona), 1965.

Jones, J. E. A model of group development. In J. E. Jones & J. W. Pfeiffer (Eds.), *The 1973 annual handbook for group facilitators*. La Jolla, Calif.: University Associates, 1973.

Jones, J. F. Group development: A graphic analysis. In J. W. Pfeiffer & J. E. Jones (Eds.), *A handbook of structured experiences for human relations training* (Vol. II, Rev.). La Jolla, Calif.: University Associates, 1974.

Tuckman, B. W. Developmental sequence in small groups. *Psychological Bulletin*, 1965, *63*, 384-399.

Group Cycles

When a group engages in the process of "moving" from its present status toward a more desirable position, it experiences both progress and setbacks along the way. The Group Cycles Model, adapted by Walt Boshear, identifies five characteristic states in a group's development that have a sequential relationship to one another.

1. *Denying the facts*. In this pregrowth state, the members actively or passively deny the existence of a problem or need for change in their group. The group may function indefinitely in the passive mode by simply avoiding confrontation of the issues. In the active mode, the members try to talk the problem away with rationalizations and other means of convincing themselves and others that the group problem does not exist. If the members individually have a strong stake in the status quo or an overriding fear of change, then the group will never move out of this stage.

2. *Blaming others*. Usually when group members are forced to pay attention to a problem or need for change, their initial response is to fix the blame. It is not unusual for the group to focus blame on the member who identifies the problem or need—the "messenger" is seen as the "cause." Frequently, in addition to assigning blame within the group, the members attempt to externalize the problem. They justify their inaction by blaming outside individuals, groups, or organizations for the problem and assigning the responsibility for action to them.

3. *Accepting responsibility*. This state is a conceptual leap from either of the first two. In this phase, the members recognize the existence of the problem, abandon their attempts to assign the responsibility elsewhere, and accept individual and mutual responsibility for producing a change. This change in orientation from past to present and future allows the resources and energies of the group to be aligned in a common direction—forward.

4. *Problem solving*. In this state, the members are engaged in gathering data, sharing information, and evaluating alternative solutions. They converge on an acceptable course of action for implementation and their objectives are toward optimizing resources. Individual capabilities are

realistically evaluated, and roles are dynamic, changing to meet the needs of the moment.

5. *Hypothesis testing*. Rarely does a group go beyond problem solving to the state where members begin to test their basic assumptions and "truths." In this final stage, members intellectually and emotionally risk themselves in conducting experiments to examine and understand themselves and the process by which they function. They simultaneously are "doing" and "aware of doing." Their trust level is high and the performance standards are self-imposed and demanding.

As Figure 29 indicates, the five group-cycle phases are sequentially related. As a group encounters personal and functional roadblocks, it can fall back to any former state. An assumption behind the model, confirmed by observation, is that groups continually and repeatedly go through these phases. As a group grows, the members learn to recognize when they are in a dysfunctional stage and move back "up" the sequence very rapidly.

DISCUSSION

We have found the Group Cycles Model useful monitoring a group's progress because it provides members with a conceptual framework and vocabulary for discussing their own process. The behavior representing each phase in the group cycle is easy to visualize and communicate.

When the group is highly task oriented, such as in team building and organization development, the model is particularly effective. It achieves the most impact if it is introduced when a group is experiencing its first major "regression." For example, the group may have (1) reached the problem-solving phase, (2) encountered a major functional problem, and (3) reverted to blaming others. At this precise point, when emotions are high and the members are sensing a loss, the model can help the group to re-establish its direction. And it can continue to provide recovery strategies for regression episodes that occur in the group's future.

To our knowledge, there is no published reference to this concept or model. It evolved in a team-building session in Las Vegas, Nevada. We do not know whether any of the participants brought all or part of the model from another source or if it was created out of the needs of the group to understand itself.

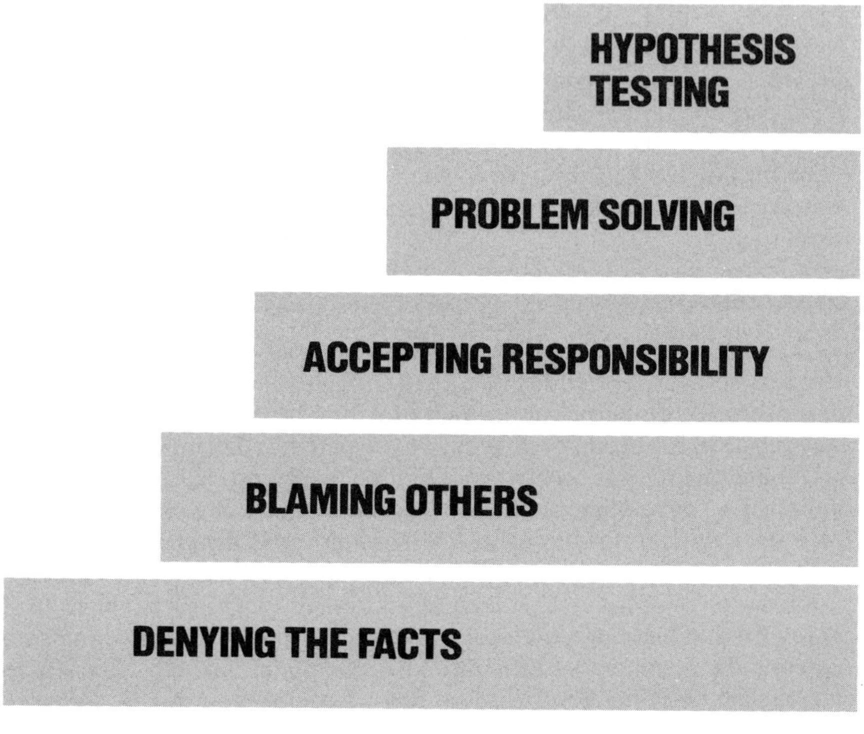

HYPOTHESIS TESTING

PROBLEM SOLVING

ACCEPTING RESPONSIBILITY

BLAMING OTHERS

DENYING THE FACTS

Figure 29. The group cycle model

CONCLUSION TO
GROUP MODELS

In the introduction to this section, we contended that there is a natural limit to group size. Our conclusion is that the world, as seen by applied behavioral scientists, is composed of a large number of intersecting groups, each no larger than about twenty people. Beyond that parameter, we enter the realms of sociology, philosophy, and other highly abstract disciplines, which we believe have little direct application to *daily living*.

A logical subsequent level of models seems to be *intergroup* models. However, our experience has shown that a group can be treated very much like an individual insofar as its interaction with other groups is concerned. The dyad and group models are generally quite sufficient for understanding intergroup behavior; all that is required is the substitution of the word *group* wherever the words *individual* or *person* appear.

It may be that groups, as such, don't really interact with one another—the interaction is between individuals who represent groups. In that capacity the individuals behave much as they always do with the added influence of the group identity, which was discussed in detail in the Behavioral Influences of Groups Model.

The previous paragraphs imply that the field of applied human behavior is bounded by a natural function—the number of *relevant interactions* that an individual or a group can maintain with other individuals or groups. The full implications of this idea are beyond us at this time. However, we are eager to expand our knowledge and understanding of this phenomenon.

With the conclusion of Part Three, then, we leave the vertical approach to models and move laterally into the considerations of individuals, dyads, and groups with special characteristics. The next section, Organization Models, considers the impact of authority and structure on an individual, dyads, and groups.

PART 4
ORGANIZATION MODELS

INTRODUCTION TO
ORGANIZATION MODELS

Most of the behavioral processes of interest within formal organizations can be studied with group-oriented models, but there remains an untended area: the behavior of individuals who find themselves in positions of formal authority. Commonly called managers, these people are typically perceived by others as playing highly structured roles in group situations.

Within the past two decades, the practice of management has earned increasing status as a legitimate social function of a high order. Management calls for abilities, strategies, and attitudes quite unlike those required to perform any more specialized jobs. Many behavioral scientists have studied managers, managing, and management, attempting to label, classify, and analyze the processes that are fundamental to the role of manager. This research, however, has produced discouraging results—only a few systematic approaches to analyzing managerial effectiveness. Many research efforts seem mired in high-order abstractions—imagined traits that are granted the legitimacy of real-world "things." Other researchers seem to accomplish little more than disproving the conjectures of previous investigators. Consequently, the enlightened layman—often a manager himself—may be left with no framework at all for organizing his thoughts about management.

Many investigators have attempted to model large-scale organizations. Their notable lack of success stems, we believe, from semantic misperception of the processes being studied. This misperception arises from the indiscriminate use of the abstract term *organization*, which people use to describe complex processes. While the term *group behavior*—if carefully used—has some validity for small groups, the term *organizational behavior* does not. An organization does not "behave" in the same sense that an individual does. Nor are organizational processes conceptually similar to those of dyads or small groups. Indeed, we define a *group* as a set of people that is small enough to allow each member to have significant interactions with all other members during the normal course of group activities. This is not possible in a large organization, such as an industrial firm, a government agency, a national fraternal society, or an academic institution.

In Part 4, we approach "organizational" processes by means of selected group-oriented models in combination with the management models. This strategy arises from the following considerations. First, most of the human processes occurring in a formal organization actually take place within small groups. For example, the typical work group in an industrial firm ranges from three to about a dozen people. The same size membership can be found in a typical problem-solving business meeting and in the top staff of a very large corporation. Even the president of the United States has a cabinet of eleven members. Therefore, although the formal leader of a large organization presides over the activities of many people, he does so by interacting with a rather small number of them—his staff. Each of the staff members interacts with a small number of other people who report to him, and so on down the formally structured chain of command. Small-group models work quite well for describing these processes. Where the *structure is highly formalized* and *functions are pronounced*, these factors become significant inputs to the various models.

Secondly, individuals who live and work in large organizations usually perceive the organization only dimly, but they clearly see their local task groups. They tend to perceive the top management of their organization as an undifferentiated general influence on *their local groups*, not on themselves as individuals. Similarly, those who occupy the formal positions of high authority tend to perceive the membership of their organizations as an undifferentiated mass of people who respond in a general sense to their direction.

These tendencies suggest a need for models that deal with the attitudes of formal leaders toward the general membership, and vice versa. The few such models that are available have been included in this section. They fall into two general classes. The first group examines the possible assumptions, attitudes, reaction patterns, convictions, and values that may influence a leader's strategies in dealing with people. The second group of models attempts to illuminate the age-old question of why people do the things they do.

Formal and Informal Organizations

The Formal and Informal Organizations Model is a general purpose framework for examining interpersonal relationships within a formally structured organization. Karl Albrecht and Walton Boshear synthesized the model from a wide variety of concepts found in the behavioral sciences literature.

Most people who live and work within the confines of a *formal* organization recognize the existence of an *informal* organization. A very common attitude is that there are many interpersonal working relationships, alliances, and "treaties" in any large organization, and without them the unit probably could not continue to function. The model implies that this contention is quite valid.

Organization Chart

The primary vehicle for describing, discussing, and *thinking about* the formal organization is the *organization chart*. Figure 30.1 shows a typical chart, with the principal types of inter-unit relationships illustrated within the structure. When an organization chart is developed, either to describe an existing organization or to plan a new one, the divisions can take several forms. For example, a typical government agency might be divided according to the various categories of services it provides. A large industrial conglomerate might be divided into major aspects of operation, such as product categories or marketing areas.

Organization charts are in such widespread use in American organizations, that they have come to dominate their thinking more than most people realize. Many people attempt to use organization charts for purposes that are far removed from the chart's basic function. They may try to describe the kind of activities that go on in an organization, to identify communication paths, or to look at intergroup activities. None of these are clearly expressed by the chart.

For the human relations practitioner an organization chart has several legitimate functions. It shows the span of control of each manager—the number of people over whom the manager has direct formal authority. Typically this ranges from three to ten, which is consistent with the

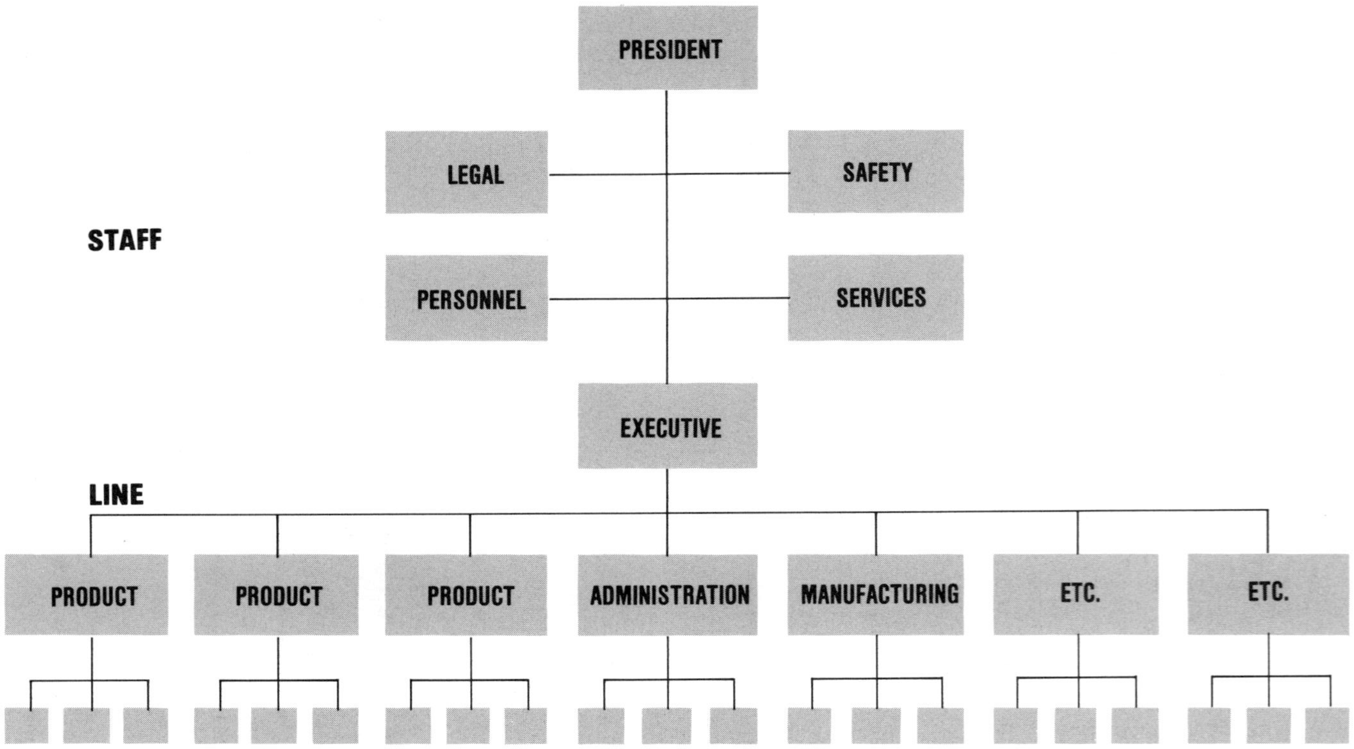

STAFF

LINE

PRESIDENT

LEGAL

SAFETY

PERSONNEL

SERVICES

EXECUTIVE

PRODUCT

PRODUCT

PRODUCT

ADMINISTRATION

MANUFACTURING

ETC.

ETC.

156

Figure 30.1. Typical organization chart

theoretical limits on group size. This span of control can reveal a great deal about the demands on the manager for continued, enforced interpersonal relationships. In fact, the formal organization chart clearly indicates only one basic aspect of the group: *authority relationships*. That is, it shows who has control and formal influence over whom. Since power, authority, and influence are such fundamental aspects of American business operations, they tend to be settled first, and attended to more frequently than any others.

The organization chart can provide some insight, but not much, into the role imposed on people in the organization. For example, when an organization is subdivided into separate marketing areas, there is often an assumption of competitiveness between the respective managers. Routine reporting systems perpetuate this because they tend to be comparative in nature.

The representation of positions in a hierarchy on the chart—some higher, some·lower—can impose on people a perception of their relative worth with regard to others. Theoretically, this relates only to their professional skill and experience, but in fact, it affects their feelings of personal worth and can heavily influence their behavior on and off the job.

If taken too much at face value, the organization chart can lead to pitfalls. For example, it could lead to the assumption that the lines of communication and authority are absolute. In fact, a message cannot be transmitted along the organizational "wires" and reach its destination intact. And an order issued at the top of an organization often will not be reflected directly by a change in the behavior of the people at the bottom.

In these respects, the formal organization chart has little to do with interpersonal interactions. It presents a very static picture of the human processes involved. To a great extent, organization charts tend to imprison the thinking of people who rely on them.

Informal Relationships

The Formal and Informal Organizations Model adds important dimensions to the analysis of human interactions within an organization. The diagrammatic representation of the model, shown in Figure 30.2, is a formal chart combined with a Venn diagram of the particular informal relationships being studied. The Venn diagram simply uses overlapping circles to represent groups of people. The areas of overlap symbolize people who belong to both of the groups represented by the circles. Often, there is no clear correspondence between the formal chart and the informal diagram. The value of comparing the two is in dealing with authority relationships within the context of interpersonal activities.

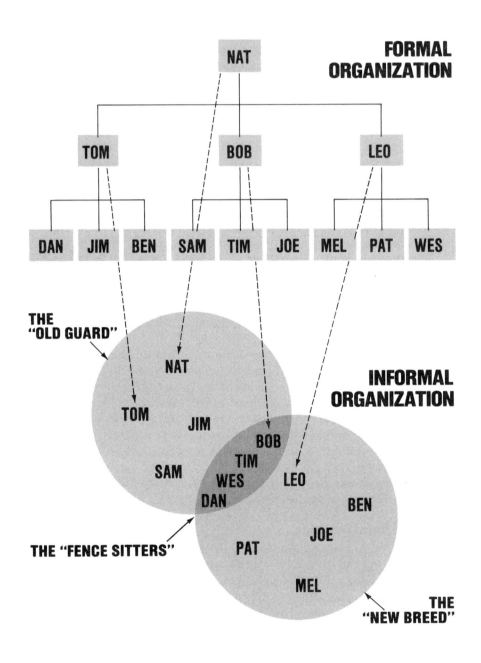

Figure 30.2.   Formal/Informal organization models

In any formal organization, there are many possible informal organizations. The relative impact of any one of these informal organizations on day-to-day functioning depends on the extent to which individuals collectively identify themselves with it, and allow it to influence their role relationships. For example, American military organizations are populated by two social classes: officers and enlisted people. These two organizations do not show up on the typical organization chart—say of a headquarters staff unit—but the personnel clearly perceive the differences. The traditions of many military organizations place extreme pressures on individuals who attempt to violate these well-defined class boundaries.

One of the most common processes within any informal organization—a process which is completely ignored by the formal chart—is the formation of *tribes*. In many instances, the tribal membership boundaries parallel certain formal organization boundaries. Certain classical "fracture lines" develop between particular functional units. For example, in many industrial companies the manufacturing people form a tribe to combat the perceived depredations of the sales tribe. This often arises because of certain inevitable differences in objectives. In their efforts to move the company's products, sales people are usually oriented to fast delivery, cost cutting, and new product configurations.

Manufacturing people, on the other hand, may be oriented to product quality, work scheduling, and standardization. Unless both functional groups acknowledge these differences, they may very well perceive each other as enemy groups.

Individuals who belong to the separate formal organizations, but who refuse to psychologically "join" either of the two tribes, may play an important part in reducing intergroup tension and rivalry. By virtue of their uncommitted status, they can function as communication facilitators.

DISCUSSION

The Formal and Informal Organization Model is useful for analyzing the social psychology of business. It is a means by which managers can escape from the restrictive influences of the formal organization chart. By acknowledging and analyzing the major influences of informal organizations, a manager can capitalize on these on-going processes to meet his objectives more effectively. For example, the organizational "grapevine," an important part of any large operation, can play a beneficial role in facilitating the informal communication of new ideas, trends, and objectives.

The primary value of the model is in its focus on the great *variety* of role relationships and their connections with the formal organization. In this sense, it serves as a general-purpose model, applicable to many situations. The model is helpful, too, in dealing with organizational politics. (In this discussion, the term *politics* is intended to mean the dynamics of authority and influence without the negative connotations usually assigned to it in the business context.)

A limitation—and an advantage—of the model is simplicity. It cannot readily be extended to the analysis of complex interactions. On the other hand, in a training situation it helps to generate discussion about social processes within a particular organization.

In a seminar/workshop setting, the model is useful for dealing with managerial communication and human relations, and it is also good for lecture work on organizational effectiveness.

SUGGESTED READINGS

Cornell, W. B. *Business Organization.* New York: Alexander Hamilton Institute, 1960.

Durand, R. *Business: Its organization, management and responsibilities.* Englewood Cliffs, N. J.: Prentice-Hall, 1964.

Galbraith, J. *Designing complex organizations.* New York: Addison-Wesley, 1973.

Jay, A. *Corporation man.* New York: Random House, 1971.

Taylor, F. W. *Principles of scientific management.* New York: W. W. Norton, 1967.

31 Effective Authority

The Effective Authority Model was developed by Walt Boshear and Karl Albrecht to examine the results of mixing different types of leadership authority in a group. The model identifies two types of authority that can vary independently: *formal* and *earned*.

Formal authority is the degree to which an individual is empowered to *direct the behavior* of others within a group. The leader's authority may be *externally* derived—assigned from outside the group—or it may be *internally* derived from a formal elective or appointive process.

Earned authority is the degree to which an individual is able to *elicit the support* of group members. Earned authority is only internally derived, that is, granted by the group members themselves.

Although formal and earned authority theoretically vary only in a positive direction from *none* to *absolute*, in practice, they vary from *none* to *high*. Both, however, have an additional direction. Authority can be granted to an individual in a positive direction from none to high, or it can be taken away by strategies designed to obstruct its operation. This obstruction produces *negative* authority. A mixture of formal and earned authority results in *effective authority*.

The degree of a leader's effective authority may be evaluated in terms of the members' functional or dysfunctional behavior in the group. Functional behavior is loosely defined as goal-supportive and dysfunctional behavior as goal-detractive. Conditions of mixed authority can be diagrammed as shown in Figure 31, and categorized for discussion, as follows:

High formal authority with high earned authority. This condition results in the maximum of leader influence from an individual who has the formal authority to direct the behavior of the individuals in the group and also has achieved a high degree of earned authority. Not only do group members respond positively to his direction, but in the absence of specific direction, their activities are oriented to the values and objectives he supports.

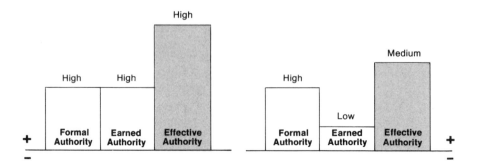

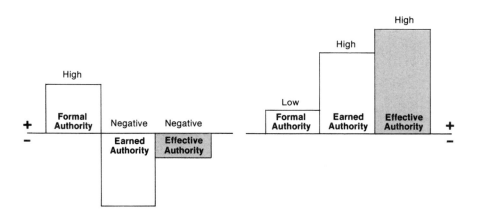

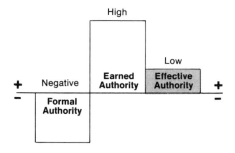

Figure 31. Effective authority model

High formal authority with low earned authority. Effective authority is reduced, although the formal authority is the same as that in the first condition. By specific direction, the leader can elicit functional behavior from the group members. But in the absence of specific direction, the members will do nothing to support the objectives or reach the established goals of the group.

High formal authority with negative earned authority. In this condition, the productive results of the leader's formal authority are completely offset by the counterproductive behavior of the group members— represented as negative earned authority. The leader is virtually ineffective in advancing the objectives of the group, and no progress is made toward group goals.

Low formal authority with high earned authority. The leader in this situation can do little formal directing of the group. However, the members have granted him a high degree of informal authority, and they engage in behavior to reach objectives he perceives as valuable. Although he has little formal authority, the leader has some effective authority because the members follow his lead.

Negative formal authority with high earned authority. In this situation, the leader is actively thwarted by the system or the organization in his exercise of formal authority. Group members, however, recognize and respect his knowledge and ability and seek his advice. Many times this activity is covert and hidden from the system to avoid negative consequences for the leader and the group members. The leader, nonetheless, has some effective authority.

The Effective Authority Model is based on the relative degrees of formal and informal authority of *one* individual. However, it can be extended to the situation in which formal authority is assigned to one individual and informal authority is earned by another. If the two authority figures have compatible objectives, their combination may result in a high degree of effective authority. In other words, the area of effective authority may be additive. If their objectives are in conflict, the two leaders may cancel most of each other's effective authority, leaving a low net effective authority.

DISCUSSION

The Effective Authority Model is an excellent tool for discussing authority and its effect. However, the model's imagery creates an almost irresistible urge to actually measure the various kinds of authority. This is totally beyond the scope or intent of the model and will lead the user into trouble. The degree of formal, earned, and effective authority can be "measured" only in a gross sense.

Our most effective use of the model has been in management development and leadership training. By introducing the concept of earned authority and its relationship to formal authority, the model provides a foundation for other models and techniques that help the manager or leader increase his effective authority and *earn* the informal authority of the group.

A powerful message can be conveyed to the management trainee with this model: formal authority can be granted to a *position* by an organization, but earned authority can be accrued only by the *individual* who occupies the position. In other words, certain formal authority is assigned by the organization chart to the position of department manager. Pete Smith acquires formal authority by virtue of his appointment to the position of department manager. The "department manager" has no earned authority. Only Pete Smith may acquire a degree of earned authority through his interpersonal relationships with the members of his staff. Understanding the distinction between formal and earned authority could lead a manager to develop deliberate strategies for learning the interpersonal skills of management.

32 Leader Effectiveness

Fred Fiedler developed the Leadership Effectiveness Model while doing research on the most effective leadership style. He arrived at the conclusion that a leader's effectiveness—the strength of his influence on the group—depends on the group situation, as well as on the leader's personality. He also identified two types of leaders and the group situations in which they are most effective. In the model, group situations are classified according to three major factors, *leader-member personal relations*, *task structure*, and *position power of the leader*, which are described as follows:

Leader-member relations indicate the relative degree of respect, admiration, trust, and affection existing between the leader and the members as a group.

Task structure determines the degree to which the group's assignments are specified. High task structure allows very little choice of what to do; low task structure requires the group to decide what to do and how to do it.

Position power is the authority vested in the leader's position. It usually is measurable in a relative sense and is perceived and acknowledged by group members.

Fiedler contends that leader-member relations play the dominant role in leader effectiveness; task structure is the second most important factor, and position power is third. All three factors must be examined to assess the quality of interaction between the leader and members of a group. For example, a leader who has poor relationships with the group members, a loosely structured task system, and low position power would probably not be very effective. On the other hand, a leader who enjoys good relationships, highly structured tasks, and high position power would probably have a high level of effectiveness in the group's operation.

Variations in the three factors constitute a scale of "favorableness" for the leader's role with the group, as shown in Figure 32. If the leader has good leader-member relations and enjoys a high degree of position power, and if the group has a high task structure, then the leader can have

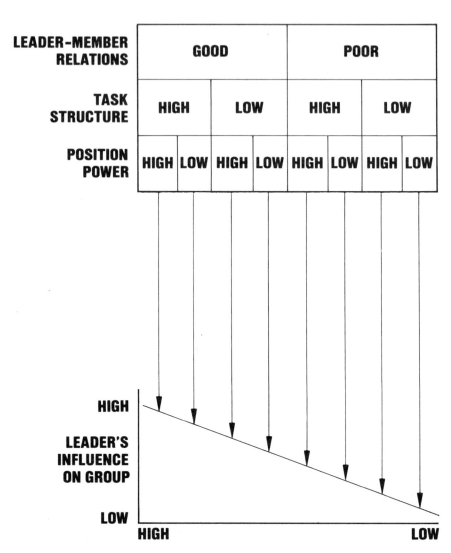

Figure 32. Leader effectiveness model
(Adapted from Fiedler 1969)

166

a high influence on the group. On the other extreme, with poor leader-member relations, low or little position power, and a low task structure, the leader will be able to exercise only a minimum influence on the group.

Under favorable circumstances, one might expect a leader to be effective, as measured by some index of group performance. However, Fiedler cites studies that point to an additional factor in leadership effectiveness. This is the matter of leadership styles, which he characterizes as either *task-oriented* or *relationship-oriented*. These studies indicate that a task-oriented leader may be highly effective in certain situations—at certain points along the continuum of favorableness—and quite ineffective in others. According to Fiedler, the task-oriented leader is more effective at the extremes of the scale—high influence or low influence as measured by the three major factors—than in the middle. Conversely, the relationship-oriented leader is more effective in the middle of the scale than at the extremes. That is, the task-oriented individual performs better in a situation of good relations, high structure, and high power, or in a situation of poor relations, low structure, and low power, than in an intermediate situation. The relationships-oriented leader, on the other hand, performs better in a situation of intermediate relations, moderate task structure, and moderate power, than he does under the high and low extremes.

Fiedler suggests that a person can improve his effectiveness as a leader by placing himself (or by being placed) in situations that favor his particular style. This theory of fitting the job environment to the leader has important implications for the management of large organizations. To maximize the potential effectiveness of individual leaders, top management can match them with appropriate work groups and even alter their authority, task, and interpersonal relations.

DISCUSSION

The Leader Effectiveness Model has a rather reassuring quality of simplicity and definiteness, which makes it simultaneously appealing and misleading. We are apprehensive of attempts to simplify the very dynamic function of leadership or define it in static form and have some serious reservations about Fiedler's model as we understand it. While hastening to affirm its value as a tool for discussion and analysis of some key aspects of leadership, we object to using the model as a measurement tool. We believe in a positive-thinking approach to modeling leadership dynamics, but in this case must point out certain conceptual traps that ensnare many investigators in this area.

One snare is the conceptualization of "leadership" as an objective characteristic of a person's existence, like hair color or physical strength.

This concept easily leads to terms like "leader effectiveness" and to attempts to assign measures to them. Because the entire concept of leadership is so highly abstract, it would make just as much sense, semantically, to discuss "followership."

A second conceptual trap lies in treating the function of leadership as if it were a static condition, rather than a process. The classification of leaders as *either* "task-oriented" *or* "relationship-oriented" is a semantic pitfall of the most primitive form. The overuse of either/or terminology can easily tempt one to *think* in an either/or fashion.

When using the Leader Effectiveness Model, we prefer to limit the conceptual framework to the basic three-axis relationship between position power, task structure, and leader-member relations.

A more interesting and fruitful subject for analysis would be helping individuals learn to function in groups, with emphasis on authority and influence *when appropriate*. Considerable exploration is needed in this area, not in search of normative structures, but in search of unifying concepts that are low enough on the ladder of abstraction to be connected with actual behavioral options available to the individual who is trying to "lead."

SUGGESTED READING

Fiedler, F. E. Style or circumstances: The leadership enigma. *Psychology Today*, March, 1969. Also in W. R. Lassey (Ed.), *Leadership and social change.* La Jolla, Calif.: University Associates, 1971.

33 Theory X and Theory Y

The Theory X and Theory Y descriptions of management philosophy, developed by Douglas McGregor, form a useful model for approximating and comparing basic assumptions about people in organizations. After much study, McGregor concluded that most American institutions, especially industrial firms and government organizations, are managed according to a traditional set of assumptions about people. These assumptions constitute a body of folklore about human behavior and motivation. McGregor referred to this set of assumptions as a "theory" of management—Theory X. Drawing on the accumulation of scientific knowledge about human behavior, he advanced an alternate set of assumptions—Theory Y. He believed that Theory Y would lead to more effective motivation and improved mental health for workers and, consequently, to better achievement of management's goals.

Theory X

Theory X represents what McGregor believed were the assumptions underlying conventional managerial policies and practices:

1. The average human being has an inherent dislike for work and will avoid it if he can.
2. Because they dislike work, most people must be coerced, controlled, directed, or threatened with punishment to get them to put forth adequate effort toward the achievement of organizational objectives.
3. The average human being prefers to be directed, wishes to avoid responsibility, has relatively little ambition, and wants security above all.
4. People are inherently self-centered and indifferent to organizational needs.
5. People are by nature resistant to change.
6. People are gullible, not very bright, and are ready dupes of the charlatan and the demagogue.

169

Although managers or supervisors rarely verbalize the Theory X assumptions, the strategies they adopt in dealing with employees often suggest that they hold the Theory X assumptions—either consciously or unconsciously. A Theory X manager probably spells out job responsibilities, directs employees closely toward objectives that he may not bother to explain to them, rewards them for conformance to narrow behavioral norms, and punishes them for deviation. These actions influence the responses of employees, but the underlying assumptions or reasons for them are seldom tested or even recognized. Most managers behave as though their beliefs about human nature are correct and require no evaluation or testing.

Theory Y

McGregor proposed another view of human nature, significantly different from Theory X, but not necessarily representing the opposite extreme. Referred to as Theory Y, this approach was based upon the following assumptions:

1. The expenditure of physical and mental effort in work is as natural for people as play or recreation.
2. External control and threat of punishment are not the only means for inducing people to work toward organizational objectives. A person will exercise self-control in the service of objectives to which he is committed.
3. The individual's commitment to objectives is dependent on rewards associated with their achievement. Rewards that satisfy needs for self-respect and personal achievement can have powerful influences on human behavior.
4. Under proper conditions, the average human being learns not only to accept responsibility but to seek it.
5. The capacity to exercise a relatively high degree of imagination, ingenuity, and creativity in solving organizational problems is widely distributed in the population.
6. Under the conditions of modern industrial life, the intellectual potentialities of the average human being are only partially utilized.

A Theory Y manager is likely to focus on the dynamics of individual behavior as the source of his strategies for mobilizing human effort toward organizational objectives. He attempts to structure the work environment—its tasks, responsibilities, and opportunities for achievement—in such a way that it offers significant rewards for employees who work toward organizational goals. He emphasizes reward rather than punishment as a means of motivating people. Figure 33 compares sets of assumptions for Theory X and Theory Y and their implications for management strategy.

A very important distinction must be drawn between the Theory Y management style and coddling employees. The latter is merely a soft Theory X approach. One Theory X manager may drive his employees because he sees them as lazy and believes this is the only way to get them to accomplish anything. Another may try to "keep them happy" with effusive praise and a "sweetness and light" atmosphere, believing he can coax them to produce. But both approaches arise from the same basic set of assumptions about man; both are essentially manipulative strategies.

The Theory Y style of managing people sets high standards and expects people to reach them. From the supervisor who has grown up under some of the Theory X influences of our culture, Theory Y demands a new and different way of dealing with people. It may also be confusing and challenging to employees who have come to expect Theory X treatment from their supervisors. Risk taking is necessary on the part of the manager, who must allow subordinates to experiment with activities that may be unfamiliar to them.

DISCUSSION

The Theory X and Theory Y Model strongly suggests that the two theories of behavior are opposing extremes. In some respects, this dichotomy may be appropriate, but in others, it may be a limitation. For example, one might be tempted to conclude that all of the assumptions of Theory X should be reversed in moving to Theory Y. But money and security may be extremely important factors in certain kinds of situations. They satisfy needs that must be attended to before the more abstract levels of needs become operative in influencing behavior. In certain kinds of situations, a Theory Y manager might consciously use pressure or coercion if he considers it the most effective overall approach. The flexibility to make these choices is basic to his effectiveness as a manager.

Actually, McGregor was trying to induce managers to examine their basic assumptions about human behavior, *whatever they might be*. He maintained that the manager's strategies for dealing with his subordinates were born of assumptions that should be consciously recognized, tested, and evaluated.

The model appeals to us as practitioners of the applied behavioral sciences because it is oriented toward effectiveness. We believe the most

MANAGER'S THEORY

ASSUMED ATTITUDE OF EMPLOYEES TOWARD:	THEORY X	THEORY Y
ORGANIZATIONAL OBJECTIVES	Indifferent to them	Will work toward them if they perceive rewards associated with doing so
RESPONSIBILITY	Will avoid it if possible Prefer to be directed	Will accept responsibility if they are rewarded for acting responsibly Capable of self-direction toward objectives that are valuable to them
WORK	Dislike all forms of work Will avoid if possible	Consider work as natural as play if they associate rewards with working
REWARDS	Want money and security More pay will produce more work	Behave in ways that seek to satisfy a variety of needs
APPROPRIATE MEANS FOR DEALING WITH EMPLOYEES	Coercion, pressure, threat of punishment Well-specified tasks and close control Pay and monetary incentives	Establish a work environment in which employees can realize recognition, challenge, satisfaction of achievement, etc.

Figure 33. Theory X and Theory Y comparison

important drawback of the Theory X approach to management is not its inhumane view of man, but the fact that it does not work well. The basic assumptions of Theory X lead to management practices that bring undesirable results: coercion brings resentment; lack of trust brings alienation and detachment; threat of punishment brings retaliation; overcontrol brings obedient, robotlike behavior. Ironically, these are all behaviors that Theory X managers complain about, which makes Theory X a kind of self-fulfilling prophecy. The employees respond with behavior that leads the manager—consciously or unconsciously—to confirm his assumptions about the nature of man.

The Theory X and Theory Y Model is simple, thought-provoking, and easy to apply. We have found it valuable as a framework for self-examination and a vehicle for seminar and workshop activities dealing with the personnel problems of management. It can be used with encounter and team-building groups for presenting new concepts in an atmopshere of experimentation and self-examination. It focuses attention on a fundamental question for the manager: "Do you make one set of assumptions about the motivations of your employees and another set of assumptions about your own motivations?"

SUGGESTED READINGS

Lassey, W. R., & Fernández, R. R. (Eds.), *Leadership and social change* (2nd ed., rev.). La Jolla, Calif.: University Associates, 1976.

McGregor, D. *The human side of enterprise.* New York: McGraw-Hill, 1960.

34 Motivation/ Hygiene Concept

The Motivation/Hygiene Concept, developed by Frederick Herzberg, provides a model for assessing a manager's options for influencing employee motivation and performance. Assumptions about employee motivation are fundamental to traditional management theory. However, Herzberg asserts that the traditional assumptions are inappropriate for the modern work force or are simply false. Probably because very few managers have thoroughly tested their assumptions, and reliable alternatives to those assumptions are not readily grasped, the folklore about motivation has become codified over the years into a body of rules about "how to handle people."

The Motivation/Hygiene Model identifies *hygiene* and *motivation* as the two categories of job factors that influence the worker, and it defines them as follows:

Hygiene. These "pain-relievers" are conditions required by the employee to maintain good social, mental, and physical health. They include pay, fringe benefits, safe and comfortable work space, and normal creature comforts.

Motivation. These "reward-producers" are conditions leading employees to apply *more* of their efforts—creative as well as purely physical—to their jobs. They include positive feedback, increased responsibility, greater opportunity, more challenging work, recognition, and increased status.

The classification of *pay* as a factor of hygiene rather than of motivation is significant; it directly opposes the "common knowledge" of management. Many organizations attempt to motivate workers with pay increases. These organizations usually construe motivation to mean simply a stepped-up level of some measureable variable, such as production rate. Another common approach to motivation is piecework pay—payment determined by the number of units the employee produces.

According to the M/H point of view, these payment techniques are hygiene factors because they do not have the effect of gaining an *increasing commitment* to job performance. Most workers have a "movable zero point"; that is, they tend to *adapt* to an increase in pay and eventually to consider it normal and appropriate. They may work at a higher production level for a short time after a raise, but unless the pyschological context of the job invites personal commitment, they eventually regress to a comfortable level of performance.

On the other hand, motivation factors are more reliable in gaining employee commitment because they are predominantly psychological in their influence. They answer needs that are common to virtually all workers. For example, most people enjoy receiving recognition for competent performance. An employee who has accomplished a challenging task will be motivated by recognition to extend himself even further.

Job situations that are psychologically toxic to employees can be considered *demotivating*. They involve conditions that exert negative influences on the workers' attitudes. Some demotivating conditions are equivalent to the absence of hygiene factors: low pay, poor fringe benefits, unrealistic performance demands, and fear of losing one's job. When hygiene factors are restored, the employee's environment returns to a maintenance level. However, as Figure 34 indicates, this still falls short of the *motivation* level.

Traditional management practitioners have for many years considered motivation as something the manager does *to* the employee. For example, a frequent question is "How can I *motivate* my employees?"—suggesting a manipulative attitude. Many of the traditional methods for motivation result in lower morale and de-motivation.

This model suggests that the only practical method for sustaining a condition of motivation is building a system of rewards into the job itself. If the employee finds his work challenging and stimulating, he is likely to devote an extra measure of effort to it. If the job environment gives him recognition and status for performing well, he is apt to extend himself. The model's focus is on the employee and his daily experiences, rather than on the manager's actions.

DISCUSSION

The Motivation/Hygiene Model implies that motivators are predominantly psychological factors, although they may include financial or material benefits. They offer perceived rewards that satisfy individual personal needs. And we contend that the great majority of human beings—except those who are seriously disturbed—possess an inner reservoir of creative energy that they want to express through activity. They will express this energy on the job, if they are not punished for doing so. The same young man who is considered lazy by his factory foreman might labor enthusiastically to remodel an old car in his spare time. The same worker who is considered deadwood in the office might labor all

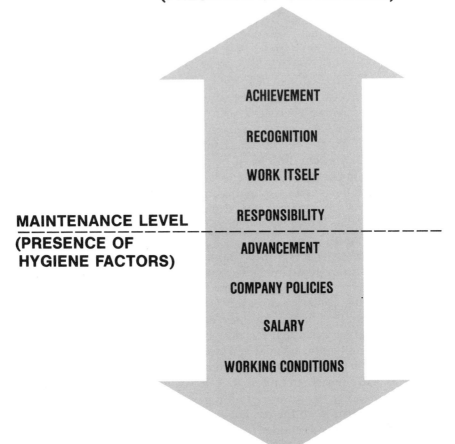

Figure 34. The motivation/hygiene concept
(Adapted from Herzberg 1966)

weekend planting roses or remodeling his house. It follows that the effective manager is one who can help his employees to release their creative energies within the job situation—channeling them toward goals that are worthwhile to themselves, as well as to the organization.

Typically, the classification of pay as a hygiene factor rather than as a motivator generates considerable argument when we present it to seminar participants. These arguments can lead to learning if ample time is planned to enable the group to thoroughly explore the issues.

We find the M/H model most useful in seminars and workshops and it has some value in team building. However, it is somewhat limited in the lecture situation because it is provocative and likely to be rejected by traditionally oriented managers.

SUGGESTED READINGS

Herzberg, F. *Work and the nature of man.* New York: The World Publishing Co., 1966.
Herzberg, F., Mausner, B., & Snyderman, B. B. *The motivation to work.* New York: John Wiley, 1967.
Maslow, A. H. *Motivation and personality.* New York: Harper & Row, 1954.
Packard, V. *The hidden persuaders.* New York: David McKay, 1957.

35 Management Style

The concept of management style has intrigued behavioral scientists for a number of years. They have devised many schemes and appropriate labels for classifying the numerous behavioral possibilities available to a manager for dealing with people within a structured organization. However, this model was developed by Karl Albrecht and Walt Boshear to define the primary *elements* of management style rather than to classify its variations.

The Management Style Model defines *style* as a pattern of managerial behavior arising from a consistent set of attitudes. It is a manager's policy of involvement in, and interaction with, group processes. Figure 35.1 diagrams this concept. A manager's style, or policy of involvement, results from choices he makes—consciously or unconsciously—about the following four factors:

Autonomy is determined by the amount of freedom a manager grants to employees; the latitude they have for deciding what to do and how to do it; and the variety of options they may exercise without his explicit permission.

Rewards are the means and methods a manager uses for rewarding (or punishing) employees for their behavior, including the strategies he uses, if any, for motivating them and the atmosphere he establishes, which leads employees to anticipate being rewarded or punished for certain kinds of behavior.

Reciprocity is the extent to which a manager allows his employees to influence his ideas, opinions, and decisions, and his inclination to listen to them and to solicit feedback.

Group process includes the extent to which a manager promotes interaction and collaboration among his employees; his facilitation of cooperation, interdependence, and group spirit; his own participation in group processes; and his strategies for employing the formal organization pattern in accomplishing objectives.

The term *style* suggests a highly personal approach to the function of

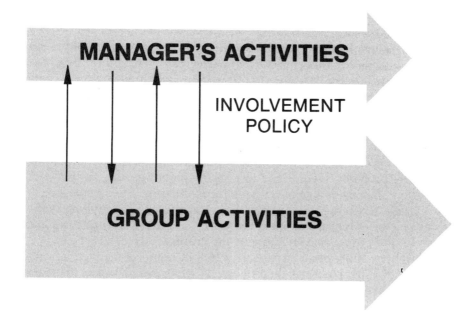

Figure 35.1.   The manager's involvement policy

management. A manager's methods and techniques for dealing with people are probably just as much a matter of personal habit and conviction as of conscious choice. The four elements of managerial behavior often are combined to form well-defined patterns displayed by individual managers. A manager's style can be identified by evaluating the relative degree to which he employs each of the four factors, using a scale of continuous variables—*tight* to *loose*. This scale is suggested by the diagram in Figure 35.2.

An example of a tight, confined style is the manager whose style can be described as "management by baseball bat." He grants little autonomy, punishes (or threatens to punish) deviations, solicits or accepts relatively little feedback from his employees, and takes an extremely role-oriented position in group activity. Always "the boss," this kind of manager limits himself to a narrow range of behavioral options.

Each of the four key factors can be applied by a manager to an extreme degree, but in excess they are counterproductive. For example, unlimited autonomy probably would lead to a disintegrated group, incapable of joint effort. Extensive use of rewards could diminish the significance of the rewards. (Extreme use of punishment constitutes a negative use of the reward factor.) Overuse of group process could result in organizational paralysis and be just as debilitating to the group as lack of structure.

It might be appropriate to assess the four elements of managerial style in terms of organizational objectives. To what extent can a manager employ the elements productively in achieving the goals of his group? It is apparent that a manager who can adapt the four key elements to an individual situation increases his range of options for interacting with his group. A variable management style may be more effective than a fixed one.

DISCUSSION

We have found this model more useful than any system of classification by labeling. Descriptive approaches are useful, especially as communication tools, but many of them fail to account for all the key elements of management style. For example, classifying his style as "charismatic" does not clearly suggest how such a manager *behaves*. Most labels of this kind are quite abstract in the semantic sense, leaving much to be desired in helping individual managers to assess their own styles. We believe the Management Styles Model meets this need quite well.

The model lacks the personal appeal of the catchy adjectives used by some classification systems, but this minor drawback can be corrected. The group leader can begin with a brief exposition of the concept of

	TIGHT ◄———		———► LOOSE
AUTONOMY	None	Strategic	Too much
REWARDS	"Stick and carrot"	Earned rewards Appropriate discipline	Lavish rewards Severe discipline
RECIPROCITY	None	Uses group ideas as resources	Wishy-washy
GROUP PROCESS	Constrained	Strategic	Over or under organized

Figure 35.2. The range of managerial style

management style, illustrating it with some of the more appealing classification terms. This can help the group to understand and appreciate the functions of the general styles model.

We consider that the principal value of the model is its comparative nature; it allows the manager to evaluate the *relative* degree to which he employs each of the four elements. Any quantitative approaches to such an abstract concept as style are strongly discouraged.

The model has been useful to us in a variety of situations. It is fairly simple to describe and lends itself well to lecturettes. It has an even greater value in the seminar and workshop setting, where the group leader can build upon it with structured experiences, instruments and other practical tools. In a structured, organizational setting, it calls attention to the need for self-examination and experimentation with one's own strategies for dealing with people.

SUGGESTED READINGS

Argyris, C. *Personality and organization: The conflict between system and the individual.* New York: Harper & Row, 1957.

Blake, R., & Mouton, J. S. *The managerial grid.* Houston, Tex.: Gulf Publishing, 1964.

Lassey, W. R., & Fernández, R. R. (Eds.). *Leadership and social change* (2nd ed., rev.). La Jolla, Calif.: University Associates, 1976.

Likert, R. *New patterns of management.* New York: McGraw-Hill, 1961.

McGregor, D. *The human side of enterprise.* New York: McGraw-Hill, 1960.

36 Managerial Grid®

The Managerial Grid, a two-dimensional model developed by Robert R. Blake and Jane S. Mouton, clarifies the behavioral dynamics that enable a manager to assess and reconcile his concern for task accomplishment with his concern for people.

Figure 36 is a simple adaptation of the Managerial Grid Model. The graph shows two variables, concern for task and concern for people, as perpendicular axes. Each axis is divided into a nine-point scale with 9 as a high degree of concern and 1 as a low degree of concern. A manager's style can be described in terms of number coordinates such as 1, 9 or 9, 1, etc. The style a manager uses for most situations can be described as his *dominant* style. Other styles that he uses as alternatives are his *back-up* styles. Of the eighty-one possible combinations within the Grid, five may be taken as most significant for discussion and analysis and have been given descriptive names:

1,1. *Impoverished*. This manager has little concern either for the task or for people. He is uncommitted to the organization's goals and has little regard for his employees. He exerts the minimum effort required to meet organizational requirements.

1,9. *Country club*. This manager adjusts the tempo of work in order to minimize the pressure on his employees. He is especially solicitous of their attitudes, morale, and well-being. His primary concern is maintaining a comfortable, friendly atmosphere.

9,1. *Task management*. This manager subordinates human concerns entirely to the accomplishment of work objectives. He measures production as carefully as possible, keeping the attention of his employees focused on performance. He has little regard for intangibles such as employee attitude, morale, or job satisfaction.

5,5. *Middle of the road*. This manager usually attempts to balance concern for task with concern for people. Over the long run, he compromises evenly, choosing actions and decisions that will strike an acceptable balance.

9,9. *Team approach*. This manager mobilizes his people to accomplish the task well, enabling them to feel personally rewarded by achieving

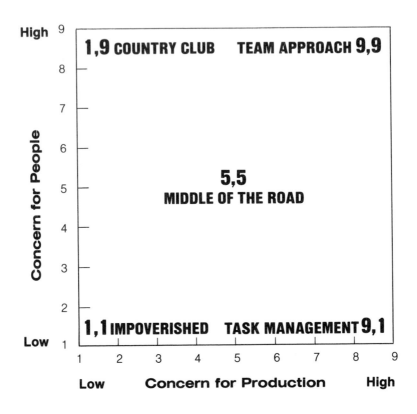

Figure 36. The Managerial Grid
(The Managerial Grid figure from *The Managerial Grid*, by Robert R. Blake and Jane Srygley Mouton. Houston: Gulf Publishing Company, Copyright © 1964, page 10. Reproduced with permission.)

the goal. He believes that interdependent functioning leads to employee satisfaction, as well as to high performance.

DISCUSSION

The geometrical representation of the Grid styles leads to the assumption that the 9,9 style should be the goal of a developing manager. However, organizational effectiveness can be achieved with a number of the possible styles. Many researchers have attempted to measure organizational performance as a function of key variables in managerial style—with generally confusing results. Some evidence suggests that a manager's high concern for the welfare of employees generally results both in improved performance and in higher morale. It is possible to achieve dramatic improvements in organizational functioning with such simple methods as training supervisors in communication skills and redesigning some jobs. On the other hand, some researchers have noted high overall performance in organizations managed by highly task-oriented individuals. We believe that organizational effectiveness is too complex to be measured by simplistic tools.

In discussions of managerial options, the Managerial Grid Model can be used to focus attention on the relationship between task orientation and people orientation. It is useful to theorists who represent all sides of the style controversy, as well as to those who stand on middle ground.

The simplicity of the Grid *diagram* may suggest that the Grid *theory* behind it is also simplistic. The full Grid theory, however, encompasses detailed combinations of styles, facades and pseudostyles, and many other aspects of managerial style assessment that make it a very comprehensive and useful theory.

We have used the Grid model most successfully in lecture situations, and in management-development seminars. It serves as a simple, convenient discussion tool for clarifying the many options available to the practicing manager and for exposing a group to the concept of management style.

SUGGESTED READINGS

Blake, R., & Mouton, J. S. *The managerial grid*. Houston, Tex.: Gulf Publishing, 1964.

Blake, R., & Mouton, J. S. An overview of the grid. In W. R. Lassey & R. R. Fernández (Eds.), *Leadership and social change* (2nd ed., rev.) La Jolla, Calif.: University Associates, 1976.

37 Leadership Continuum

The Leadership Continuum Model directs attention to the degree of authority exercised by a leader over a group. The fundamental concepts of this model have been observed and discussed by William R. Lassey, Robert Tannenbaum, and many others in the applied behavioral sciences. The model proposes a continuum, as shown in Figure 37, with points representing the characteristics of the leader's authority style. At one extreme is the *autocrat*, a leader who exercises the limit of his authority over a group. He allows members no freedom to make decisions or engage in activities that he has not specifically directed. At the other extreme on the continuum is the *abdicrat*, a leader who allows total freedom for his group. He does not provide any direction to the group. In between these two extremes are varying leadership styles, known by many labels but grouped to some degree as *democratic* leadership.

An underlying assumption of the model is that a leader may choose to behave in a manner represented by any point along the continuum. When a leader is making a decision regarding an appropriate style of leadership for his group, the following considerations are important:

- The degree of trust or confidence in the group;
- The leader's confidence in himself (or his fear of losing power);
- The degree of security the leader has in relationship with his own superiors;
- The value systems of the leader;
- The nature of the task or function of the group; and
- The objectives the leader wants to accomplish.

Greater use of leadership authority tends to depend on:

- Low trust or confidence in the group;
- Fear of losing power;
- Fear of peer or supervisor disapproval; and
- A value system arising from an authoritarian background.

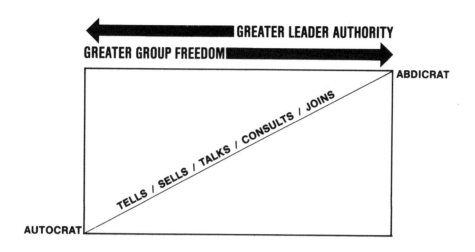

**Figure 37. The leadership continuum
(Adapted from Lassey 1971)**

Less use of authority tends to depend on:

- High trust and confidence in the group;
- Confidence in self;
- Security in relationships with peers and supervisors; and
- A value system arising from a democratic background.

Each of the styles of leadership represented along the authority continuum may be the most effective under certain conditions. For example, a leader would not consult with his subordinates about smoking in a dangerous area. And it would be ridiculous for a leader to consider "directing" higher morale or motivation.

DISCUSSION

The Leadership Continuum Model clarifies a key concept of leadership; the leader can choose the degree to which he exercises his authority over a group. Unfortunately, this leads directly to a conclusion that cannot be supported in practice: the leader has *sole* control over this decision. Exercising authority is a complex function, strongly influenced by the degree to which a group will *allow* its leader to exercise his authority. The group has an "authority," too, but the model fails to take this into account.

Our most frequent use of the model has been in learning situations with people who are facing a leadership or supervisory role for the first time. Although this model has powerful implications, its concepts are so fundamental that they appear obvious to many group participants. The model can best be demonstrated through structured experiences that allow a person to experience and experiment with various leadership methods until they come to life for him.

SUGGESTED READINGS

Lassey, W. R. Dimensions of leadership. In W. R. Lassey (Ed.), *Leadership and social change*. La Jolla, Calif.: University Associates, 1971.

Tannenbaum, R., & Schmidt, W. H. How to choose a leadership pattern. *Harvard Business Review*, May-June, 1973, 162-164, 166-168. (Also in Lassey, 1971, and in Lassey & Fernández, 1976.)

CONCLUSION TO
ORGANIZATIONAL MODELS

The models in Part 4 represent, in our our opinion, important contributions to an understanding of the human process of organizations. At the same time, they merely whet the appetite, and offer a tantalizing possibility for behavioral modeling. This is the possibility of developing a new lore of humanitarian management—one that can replace the now obsolete scientific management developed at the turn of the nineteenth century.

Primarily, these models are valuable for improving communication about behavior in situations where some form of authority relationship exists. In our work with management development groups, the models have been useful for conveying new concepts of creative management. They help the participants to study and reflect upon their own attitudes and assumptions about human behavior. They are also fairly portable,—that is, they become the conceptual property of the participant. He can take them with him in his management activities and use them when thinking about his strategies for dealing with people.

We believe much more investigation is needed in this important area, but to be fruitful, it must center on managerial *dynamics*, rather than on static, descriptive approaches. For example, one neglected area of investigation is managerial learning. Many managers will enthusiastically experiment with new concepts, if they have a framework—a model—for organizing what they learn.

An important aspect of managerial learning is *in-the-job learning*. This term refers to the capability of the practicing manager to sense the human environment, to perceive himself as a part of it, to monitor the results of his own behavior, and to adapt his approaches to what he learns. This concept focuses on growth and change *in the manager himself*, as an integral part of his adaptation to his social function.

There is also a need for models that deal with the responses of a new manager to his strange and demanding new environment. In most of the work done to date, the manager is represented as a fixed behavioral entity who brings a rigidly defined behavioral repertoire to the management situation. This approach ignores a very large class of management problems. Clearly, there is much work to be done.

PART 5

PROBLEM-SOLVING MODELS

INTRODUCTION TO
PROBLEM-SOLVING MODELS

When an individual, dyad, or group is actually or potentially in trouble, a unique set of strategies is required. These strategies are oriented toward staving off or getting out of trouble, calling for at least a temporary change in behavior—a new course of action.

Most of the models in the other parts of this book seem to assume that a person is either getting along all right or wants to get better. With few exceptions, they are not concerned with the person who is either dissatisfied with his current situation or is actively headed in a direction that is objectionable to him.

For most people, the mere presence or prediction of a problem causes changes in their behavior. In the absence of deliberate strategies for deciding on a new course of action, these revised behaviors may actually worsen a situation. People who are in trouble need good tools for understanding the nature of their problem situation, for making decisions about their course of action, and for managing the new direction once they have chosen it.

Problems usually are not clear to the individuals who have them. It is difficult to isolate *the* problem and its related components. Even if this is possible, the selection and implementation of a solution involves degrees of physical or psychological risk. Familiar patterns of behavior are safer. In a problem situation, a person is torn between the need to change and the desire to maintain the old patterns. This conflict results in strong emotions and anxieties, which impose upon the cognitive processes that are required to make workable decisions. If the problem is sufficiently severe, cognitive "paralysis" may even result.

When the solution to a problem must be reached in conjunction with other people, additional factors come into play. To allow others, even in part, to "decide one's fate" requires a high degree of trust. Frequently, people are thrown together with strangers for the purpose of solving a problem. Before the problem, when things were going well, these people may have had no reason to interact. The existence of an actual or potential problem brings them together. Because they may all have to live with the solution, each has a high stake in the process; conflict can result, with each person fighting for his own solution.

Some of the things mentioned here are included within the scope of other models already presented. There remains, however, a class of models that seem to be formulated specifically for the problem situation. These are the models we have included in this section.

 **Planned
Renegotiation**

This model is based on the premise that relationships in a social system—a two-person association, a group, an organization, or a community—seldom proceed exactly as planned or expected. John J. Sherwood and John C. Glidewell describe the probable cycle of relationships and suggest a strategy for anticipating and controlling change. They describe the following systematic phases for the relationship cycle:

Sharing information and negotiating expectations. Whenever two or more people begin an association, no matter how brief, they exchange information about themselves. From this information, they begin to predict what they can expect from one another and how their association will proceed. Uncertainty is diminished by these negotiated expectations.

Commitment. As the participants in an association begin to understand their respective roles and their shared expectations, they make commitments to one another. These commitments may be strong or weak, but they represent the agreements by the parties to live up to the expectations.

Stability and productivity. Once commitments are made and the participants understand the behavior expected of them, their relationship becomes stable. Energy can be turned from the relationship toward productivity, generally with each person performing in accordance with the shared expectations.

Disruption. It is assumed that a disruption eventually occurs in the stability of any association. The disruption may be internal to the association—one party or the other is not performing in accordance with expectations—or it may arise from some external source, such as the addition of a new person to the group.

When their expectations of an association are disrupted, the participants become uncertain. Their uncertainty is accompanied by anxiety, and the social system of their association is open to change. To relieve their anxiety, the participants might do any of the following:

- Return to phase one to share information and negotiate new expectations;

195

- Terminate the association; or, most likely,
- Return to the way things were before the disruption.

The Planned Renegotiation Model offers an alternative course of action. It recommends that an association anticipate disruption and plan for renegotiation of the original expectations. In this way, the participants do not have to make important renegotiations under the stress of uncertainty and anxiety *after* the disruption, but address these issues as a part of the stable process.

The question of renegotiation should be raised whenever an individual feels a *pinch* in the association. A pinch, a warning signal of possible disruption, is included in the cycle diagrammed in Figure 38.

DISCUSSION

The Planned Renegotiation Model offers a strategy for staying out of trouble rather than getting out of trouble. When we present the model in the learning environment it receives mildly interested attention, but later, those who have implemented the concepts report exciting results. Participants have returned to praise this model as one of the principal skills they could immediately put to work.

In experimental situations, we have used the model to teach process observation and to practice sharing process information. It seems to provide a useful framework for participants to communicate about their relationships. In one session, the word *disruption* was used by some dyads to signal each other that they should "take a process discussion break." On several occasions when a group was in the anxiety state, we have used this model to clarify the situation and the options for the future.

Although the model is complex to sketch on a chalkboard or flipchart, its labels can easily be abbreviated without losing the key points.

SUGGESTED READINGS

Harrison, R. Role negotiation: A tough-minded approach to team development. In W. W. Burke & H. A. Hornstein (Eds.), *The social technology of organization development*. Fairfax, Va.: Learning Resources Corporation/NTL, 1971.

Harrison, R. Role negotiation: A tough-minded approach to team development. In W. W. Burke & H. A. Homstein (Eds.), *The social technology of organization development*. Fairfax, Va.: Learning Resources Corporation/NTL, 1972. Reissued: La Jolla, Calif.: University Associates, 1976.

Sherwood, J. J., & Glidewell, J. C. Planned renegotiation: A norm-setting OD intervention. In W. W. Burke (Ed.), *New technologies in organization development: 1* (Originally *Contemporary organization development: Conceptual orientations and interventions*, Arlington, Va.: NTL Institute, 1972). La Jolla, Calif.: University Associates, 1975. Also in J. E. Jones & J. W. Pfeiffer (Eds.), *The 1973 annual handbook for group facilitators*. La Jolla, Calif.: University Associates, 1973.

Sherwood, J. C. & Scherer, J. J. A model for couples: How two can grow together. In *Small Group Behavior*, 1975, *6* (1), 14.

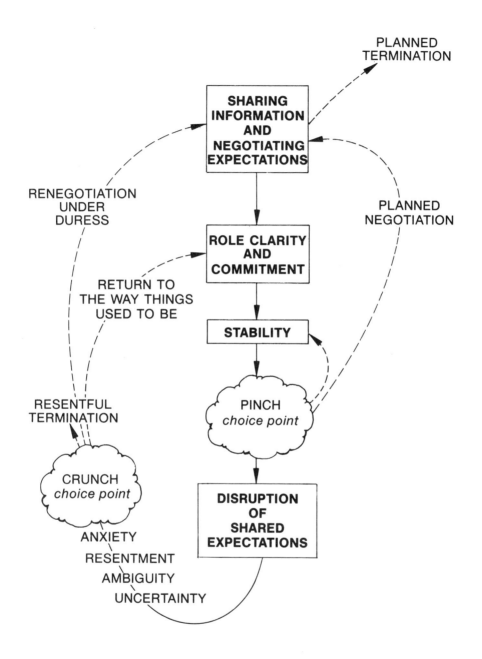

Figure 38. Planned renegotiation
(Adapted with permission of John J. Sherwood)

 **Strategies of Change**

After observing that the problem of change was approached in numerous ways by individuals, groups, and organizations, Kurt E. Olmosk isolated eight prevalent strategies of change. Those strategies and their related assumptions are described by the Strategies of Change Model as follows:

Fellowship. If people have good, warm interpersonal relations, all their other problems will be minor.

Political. If all the really influential people agree to do something, it will be done.

Economic. If people have enough money or material wealth, they can buy anything or any change they want.

Academic. People are rational. If enough facts are presented to them, they will change.

Engineering. If their environment or surroundings change, people have to change.

Confrontation. If enough anger can be mobilized to force people to look at the problems around them, the required changes will be made.

Military. Those who possess enough physical force can make people do anything.

Applied behavioral science. Most problems are complex and overdetermined. A combination of approaches is usually required.

As indicated in Figure 39, each of the strategies has its own characteristic approach to influencing people, and each has its benefits and drawbacks. Eight change strategies are discriminated and defined by the model, but in practice they are seldom used in their pure form. Usually, an individual or group employs a "mixed" style in attempting to bring about change. Certain types of individuals and groups adopt one of the change strategies as their predominant approach (although they may add modifications based on other strategies).

Fellowship. Churches, volunteer organizations, and other groups with limited power.

	INFLUENCE METHOD:	GOOD AT:	CHRONIC PROBLEMS:
FELLOWSHIP CHURCHES, VOLUNTEER ORGANIZATIONS, AND OTHER GROUPS WITH LIMITED POWER.	Relations	Mobilizing initial energy Getting people interested	Actual implementation Maintaining long run commitment is hard
POLITICAL THOSE ALREADY IN POWER.	Perceived power	Mobilizing power Implementing	Maintaining credibility Fighting backlash
ECONOMIC CORPORA- TIONS AND THE VERY WEALTHY.	Perceived wealth	Implementing deci- sions once made	Maintaining change or satisfaction
ACADEMIC OUTSIDERS. PEOPLE IN STAFF POSITIONS.	Knowledge and expertise	Finding causes Presenting relevant information	Implementation Getting people's attention
ENGINEERING TOP MANAGEMENT.	Change structure or task	Insuring compatibility of change with environment	Gaining acceptance Time consuming Difficult to control structure
CONFRONTATION REVOLU- TIONARY STUDENTS. THE POOR UNIONS.	Emotion	Gaining attention and publicity Raising issues	Finding alternatives Dealing with backlash
MILITARY MILITARY. POLICE. "WEATHER- MEN."	Force, fear	Keeping order	Rebellion Can never relax
APPLIED BEHAVIORAL SCIENCE HUMAN RELATIONS CONSULTANTS, ORGANIZATION DEVELOPMENT CONSULTANTS.	Thoughtful Involvement	Using information and resources	Being understood Not appearing wishy-washy

Figure 39. Strategies of change (Adapted from Olmosk 1972)

Political. Those already in power.

Economic. Corporations and the very wealthy.

Academic. Outsiders, people in staff positions.

Engineering. Top management.

Confrontation. Dissident students, unions.

Military. Military, police, revolutionary "Weathermen."

Applied behavioral science. Human relations consultants, organization development consultants.

Each of the strategies, used to the exclusion of others, leads to certain types of problems. These problems worsen if individuals or groups persist in trying to bring about change by intensified application of the same strategy.

DISCUSSION

The Change Strategies Model comprehensively catalogues the options available for effecting change. It has helped us convey to groups— especially management groups—that they have limited their approach to the problem of change. And it provides specific guidance for the selection of more appropriate styles for different situations.

With its large amount of data, this model is difficult to diagram for a group, so we frequently hand out a printed page to seminar or workshop participants. However, this technique makes the model somewhat less portable than others. If it is appropriate to use the model extemporaneously, we usually list the eight strategies with their associated influence methods, and then let the group develop the associated benefits, drawbacks, and related assumptions. Used in this manner, the model can lead a group to an in-depth examination of the available strategies for effecting change.

SUGGESTED READING

Olmosk, K. E. Seven pure strategies of change. In J. W. Pfeiffer & J. E. Jones (Eds.), *The 1972 annual handbook for group facilitators*. La Jolla, Calif.: University Associates, 1972.

40 Decision Cycle

The Decision Cycle Model was developed by Nena and George O'Neill to illustrate the cyclic nature of decision making and to emphasize the importance of continual reassessment of one's decisions.

The model offers some important concepts concerning the making and implementing of decisions. First, the decision process is represented, not as something people do once in a while, but as a continuing process. Second, it points out that the decision process is an internal function. Decision making has no impact on the world outside the individual until he makes a commitment and takes some action to change environmental circumstances. Last, when reconsidering a previous decision, an individual can re-evaluate two sources of information—his *internal* thoughts and feelings, and the *external* environment, as perceived by his senses. It is important to continually recheck these sources. The basic decision cycle, diagrammed in Figure 40, has the following stages:

Sensation. An individual's senses are constantly being bombarded by external occurrences in his environment. Only a small portion of this information about the world is actually received, or selectively responded to, by the receptor cells of the senses and transmitted to the brain. As far as an individual is concerned, this sensory input represents the *environment*.

Interpretation. An individual's sensory impressions do not mirror the external world. Sensory information is processed—compared with the information already stored in the memory from prior experiences—and interpreted—given meaning. This meaning (impressions, conclusions, assumptions, etc.) is unique to each person because his sensory experiences are unique. Sensory experience is influenced by his feelings—past and present, experiences, expectations, values and other learned preferences. Frequently a person sees what he wants to see, or hears what he expects to hear.

Feeling. Emotions, both new and remembered, play an important role in modifying what is sensed and thought. The same sensory input can be

201

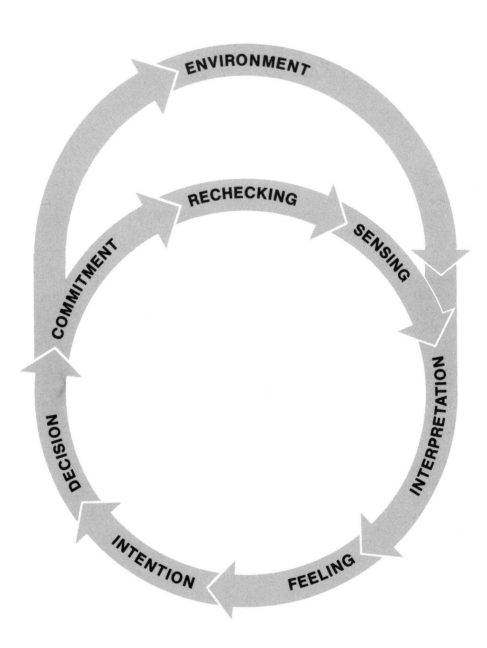

Figure 40. The decision cycle

(Adapted from *Shifting Gears: Finding Security in a Changing World* by Nena O'Neill and George O'Neill. Copyright © 1974 by Nena O'Neill and George O'Neill. Reprinted with permission of the publisher, M. Evans.)

an entirely different experience when a person is very angry, excited, or depressed, than it is when he is relatively calm. Frequently, the existence and influence of strong feelings is denied or repressed because of social pressure.

Intention. Sensory input, thoughts, and feelings are followed, sometimes simultaneously, by intentions. Although these intentions represent the wishes of the individual, many of them never have any effect on his behavior. They simply represent desires, needs, or inferences resulting from the other processes that preceded them.

The individual's sensory experiences, thoughts, feelings, and intentions represent all the information that is available to him for making large and small decisions. From this data more intentions are formulated, becoming internal pressures for the individual to modify his behavior toward bringing about more desirable circumstances.

Decision. A continuing stream of decisions are made by the individual in response to his intentions. Most of these decisions are not acted upon, and they pass out of consciousness. However, when the person is highly involved in particular decisions, they are converted into behavior.

Commitment. When an individual takes action on a decision, he has made a commitment to that decision. The results of his action generally have some impact on the environment, causing a change—however small. This change in the environment stimulates the person's senses and the cycle continues.

This model implies that the human information system is constantly feeding the decision-making process with data from three sources—senses, thoughts, and feelings; these modified by the individual's values, result in decisions. The commitment step is optional. Before making a commitment, people can recycle for more data as long as they desire.

DISCUSSION

This model distinguishes between making a decision and making a commitment. This distinction suggests a useful strategy: taking action to indicate genuine commitment to a change can facilitate the processing of that change.

The model clearly identifies intention and decision making as internal processes and commitment as an external process. And it suggests that an open channel be maintained to both the external and internal data for use in reassessing and revising behavior.

The Decision Cycle Model is simple, easy to present, and it stimulates active interest in discussion and experimentation. It is an excellent introduction to structured experiences that bring to life the sensing, thinking, and feeling functions of the cycle. It also provides a rationale for enhancing skills in each of these important areas so that more and more reliable data become available for decision making.

SUGGESTED READING

O'Neill, N., & O'Neill, G. *Shifting gears: Finding security in a changing world.* New York: M. Evans, 1974.

 **Decision Styles**

The Decision Style Model describes prevalent decision styles and suggests that the decision style chosen should be appropriate to the type of problem being confronted. Rick Roskin developed the model from research done by Norman R. F. Maier. Maier found two dimensions to be important in appraising the potential effectiveness of a decision:

- The objective *quality* or effectiveness of the decision.
- The subjective *acceptance* of the decision by those who must execute it.

Normally, and regardless of the nature of the problem, an individual will pay more attention either to quality or to acceptance. The proportion or degree of these two factors in the decision-making process determines the decision style. The four decision styles described by the model are:

Command. Using the available information, the leader makes the decision without involving the person or persons who will be executing the decision.

Consensus. The persons affected by the decision are brought together and a group decision evolves from shared information and ideas. The decision is acceptable in some degree to all group members.

Consultation. The leader makes the decision after consulting with individuals, but without bringing them together as a group.

Convenience. The leader chooses whatever method is easiest at the time the decision is required. No special consideration is given to finding the best method.

Figure 41 matches each of the four decision styles with their characteristic combinations of quality and acceptance. The model does not presume that *only* the two factors are to be considered by a leader in selecting a decision style. Other factors such as time, capability of subordinates, and the trust level in the group must be considered as well.

Regardless of the quality and acceptance factors, time constraints may require the use of the command mode. If the trust level in a group is low, a consensus-type decision may be very time consuming. Under conditions

THIS PROBLEM TYPE ➡ **SUGGESTS** ➡ **THIS DECISION STYLE**

$\dfrac{Q}{A}$ Quality more important than acceptance ⟶ **COMMAND**

$\underline{QA}$ Quality and acceptance both are important ⟶ **CONSULTATION**

$\dfrac{A}{Q}$ Acceptance more important than quality ⟶ **CONSENSUS**

$\overline{QA}$ Neither quality nor acceptance is important ⟶ **CONVENIENCE**

Figure 41. Decision style selection
(Adapted from Maier 1963)

of high trust, however, consensus decisions can be acceptable and of high quality. If the trust level in the group is high, then a consultive decision style may be very effective for achieving acceptable decisions of high quality.

DISCUSSION

For a number of years, behavioral scientists have been labeling leadership styles with three or four descriptive words, but little has been said, succinctly, about the techniques for selecting the most effective style. Although it is oversimplified, we applaud this model because it attempts to translate theory into strategy.

The principal drawback to the Decision Styles Model is its implication that decision-style selection can be reduced to a formula. However, its major advantage is the suggestion that the leader need not always operate from uncertainty. It offers hope that some aspects of leadership can be subjected to scientific discipline, rather than being considered as functions of art or instinct.

This model has significant value in leadership, management, and supervisory programs because it introduces the idea that leadership can be learned. Frequently we have had to spend much of a group's time in simply breaking down the conviction held by many members that "leaders are born, not made." Now this model takes us over that obstacle, and the group can spend its time more effectively in developing skills and experimenting with methods.

SUGGESTED READINGS

Maier, N. R. F. *Problem-solving discussions and conferences: Leadership methods and skills.* New York: McGraw-Hill, 1963.

Roskin, R. R. Decision-style inventory. In J. E. Jones & J. W. Pfeiffer (Eds.), *The 1975 annual handbook for group facilitators.* La Jolla, Calif.: University Associates, 1975.

Force-Field Analysis

The Force-Field Analysis Model was advanced by Kurt Lewin as a framework for problem solving and for effecting planned change. Lewin identified pressures or forces in an organizational system that either strongly support the openness that is necessary for change or strongly resist it.

In this model, the term *force* does not refer to a tangible, physical force, but serves as a metaphor for a broad range of influences on the interpersonal functioning in the group. For example, organizational traditions can exert strong pressures on an individual's behavior. The fact that something "has never been done before" or "has always been done this way" restrains certain people from experimenting with new ways. Prejudice, preference for certain problem-solving approaches, or distrust of others may lead some individuals to irrationally oppose a new course of action. Other influences include economic factors, interracial misunderstandings, sex-role stereotypes, division of responsibilities, personality characteristics of key figures in the organization, and rivalry between individuals or tribal-like groups. These factors can be either *driving* forces or *restraining* forces, depending on the situation and the kind of change that is desired.

The simplest representation of the model, shown in Figure 42, portrays *restraining forces* and *driving forces* arrayed against each other within a *force field*. The line of interaction between these two forces symbolizes current status. The model implies that if the hoped-for change is not coming about, then the restraining forces are collectively stronger than the driving forces. The diagram enables a person to analyze the various forces, and to develop strategies for *causing* change.

The following procedure is used when applying the Force-Field Analysis Model:

1. Specify the change desired, using concrete, measurable terms;
2. List all the factors that may influence the situation;
3. Sort the list into the two categories of driving and restraining forces;
4. Array the two lists on the force-field diagram and label them for reference.

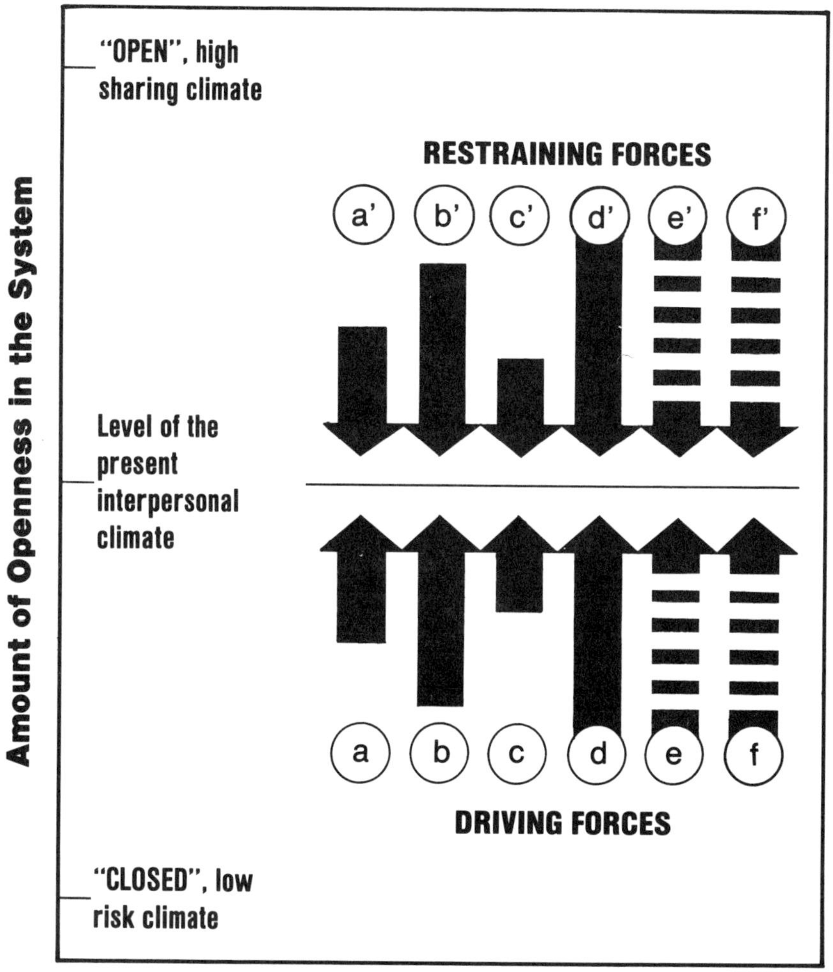

**Figure 42. The force-field analysis model
(Adapted from Spier 1973)**

A change can be stimulated by strengthening the driving forces, by weakening the restraining forces, or both. The model enables a person to analyze the forces one by one, and to identify individual strategies for dealing with each.

An effective way to deal with a restraining or resisting force is to convert it to a driving or helping force. For example, if an individual who opposes a change can discover that it offers significant benefits to him, and that he may have overestimated its negative impacts, he may change from an opponent to a supporter. This has the double effect of eliminating a force from the restraining side of the field, and adding one to the driving side.

DISCUSSION

The Force-Field Model is one of the simplest, yet most useful, schemes we have found for problem solving. In organization development, we frequently employ it to clarify our thinking about change strategies, and to communicate with executives in the initial phase of gaining their commitment to the concept of planned change. The simple elegance of the model makes it appealing to individuals who see themselves as problem-solvers. People find it exciting because it clarifies certain concepts they have been trying to deal with on an unconscious level.

The model is useful for implementing a new *management by objectives* (MBO) program in a large organization. The most common cause of failure in MBO systems seems to be passive resistance by the organization's people. Many planners are guilty of designing an MBO system in secret, and then suddenly inflicting it upon the organization. In such a case, they usually must spend one to two years overcoming organizational resistance before the system begins to take root—if it ever does. More often, the leaders of the organization suffer from a limited attention span, and give up on MBO as an unworkable system. In such a situation, the Force-Field Analysis Model enables a manager to change focus from the "MBO system " to the people within the organization who must live with the system and make it work. With this new perspective, he can replan his strategy to eliminate what are perceived as threats to employees' job stability. He can consider their needs and interests, and give sufficient time and attention to familiarizing them with the system. Instead of trying to overcome resistance, he can neutralize much of it by changing the resisting forces to helping forces.

The model generates considerable interest, and provides a simple idea to which the lecturer can refer frequently. In workshops and seminars, the model effectively supports case-study activities. We frequently use it for discussing the total response to a planned change, and for identifying effective change strategies.

In the encounter or growth-group setting, the model becomes a powerful tool for self-insight. It helps to answer the question, "What am I doing to keep myself the way I am?" The individual who is looking for strategies to facilitate personal change can consider himself as the primary force field, with various internal and external factors contending to drive and restrain the desired change.

A valuable tool for semistructured situations, the model can be used to lead in to more intensive experiences. It is also useful to some extent in discussing the progress of the group and in identifying blocks to continued advancement.

SUGGESTED READINGS

Lewin, K. Quasi-stationary social equilibria and the problem of permanent changes. In W. G. Bennis, K. D. Benne, & R. Chin (Eds.), *The planning of change*. New York: Holt, Rinehart and Winston, 1969.

Spier, S. S. Kurt Lewin's "force field analysis." In J. E. Jones & J. W. Pfeiffer (Eds.), *The 1973 annual handbook for group facilitators*. La Jolla, Calif.: University Associates, 1973.

 **Life Planning**

The individual who wants to achieve maximum satisfaction of his needs within the framework of his value system will probably have to plan his life accordingly. Karl Albrecht and Walt Boshear offer guidance toward that objective in their Life Planning Model. The model represents life planning as the following three-part process, preferably with all three activities taking place simultaneously, as diagrammed in Figure 43.

Self-Assessment: taking stock of one's life; understanding the sources of one's motivations; recognizing one's special potentials and acknowledging the blocks to their actualization.

Self-Motivation: creating a personal sense of direction; finding worthwhile challenges and goals to work for; settling upon specific desires that one can try to fulfill.

Self-Management: making written plans and committing oneself to action; monitoring progress toward measurable goals and setting new goals as they are necessary; forming the habit of working toward specific goals; holding oneself accountable for results.

This model rests upon several fundamental axioms. First, each individual in a normal social environment has the *freedom* and *responsibility* for making choices about what to do with his own life. This amounts to an *executive function* in his life. Many people flounder about in frustration, disillusionment, and despair because they have abdicated their executive function to external agencies such as The Job, The Family, The Marriage, Society, and a host of others. When a person assumes this function for himself, he becomes free to negotiate his relationships with the people and institutions in his life.

Second, the model represents the totality of an individual's life as a *process*, not as a static condition. All "normally" functioning human beings seek to structure their activities, so that they can find life rewarding or, at least, minimally punishing. People seek meaningful *activity*, not *conditions*. An American aphorism, "Happiness is a direction—not a place," suggests that goals are not necessarily rewarding in themselves, but it is the *achieving* of goals that constitutes the satisfaction. This line of reasoning implies that life planning should be oriented to meaningful action, that is, activity that serves to satisfy individual needs.

Values Needs Resources

Commitments
Actions

Objectives
Results

Figure 43. Life planning model

213

A third axiom of the model states that self-assessment, self-motivation, and self-management are *continuous* processes. This means that practical techniques for carrying out these functions must allow for continuous re-evaluation and revision. As the individual grows, his values may shift and his objectives may change. His life planning techniques must support this process, rather than hinder it. An individual can apply the Life Planning Model by breaking down each of the three phases into several specific operations.

Self-Assessment

1. Identifying one's *needs;* evaluating their relative intensity and priority; analyzing the interaction or conflicts between needs and one's mechanisms for satisfying them.
2. Clarifying one's *values;* establishing the ethical boundaries within which one can pursue need satisfaction.
3. Identifying one's *resources;* acknowledging skills, attitudes, physical attributes, intellect, personality features, finances, and other strengths one can capitalize on.

Self-Motivation

1. Selecting *objectives;* specifying one's sense of direction; spelling out major accomplishments or challenges one wishes to undertake.
2. Specifying desired *results;* identifying specific conditions, measures, material results, or personal judgments to be taken as evidence that selected objectives are being met.

Self-Management

1. Converting results to measurable *goals;* selecting intermediate checkpoints and specific accomplishments that constitute milestones in achieving the objectives.
2. Making *plans* for reaching the selected goals; giving structure to one's activities to ensure the achievement of the goals within the planned time period.
3. Taking *action* to reach the goals; engaging in activity that leads to the chosen goals; developing patterns of behavior that are highly goal-directed; structuring daily activities enough to accomplish goals as a part of living, but not as arbitrary self-discipline.

The process of self-assessment in this model does not include identifying one's weaknesses. The tendency to weigh "strengths" and "weaknesses" may result in a preoccupation with what one "can't" do. It opens the way for an individual to evade responsibility for his own life. People can capitalize on their *strengths*, not on their deficiencies.

Two common psychological mechanisms that operate to impede the processes of life planning are (1) self-defeating habit patterns, and (2) fear of becoming accountable, especially to oneself. The first problem can be overcome by diligently replacing energy-dissipating habits with habits that focus energy and support goals. The most important habit to form is the habit of setting specific goals and achieving them. An individual can begin with small, easily attainable goals, methodically establishing them and working to accomplish them, until he is well-conditioned to the goal habit.

The second resistance mechanism, however, may present great difficulty for an individual because it sabotages the very process of life planning. The fundamental premise of life planning is *personal accountability*—spelling out what one expects of oneself. People who are dissatisfied with their lives use many complaints to disguise their rejection of accountability. They must acknowledge and overcome this avoidance mechanism if they are going to manage their own lives.

The individual who has difficulty in getting started on a goal-oriented program can adopt the strategy of choosing only one goal: compiling a set of meaningful goals. He can allow as much time as he feels he needs to come to terms with the basic issues in his life, provided he establishes a specific *deadline* for doing so. This in itself is goal-directed behavior.

An important element of life planning is the need for *tangible evidence* of the process. This can be provided by a written plan used by a person to reaffirm, monitor, and guide his efforts toward specific goals. A plan that is only recorded in one's head has little value in self-management. In order to focus energy toward his own best interests, a person must clearly establish what those interests are. Faced with day-to-day choices among his many possible activities, he must select those that lead toward his goals. To do this effectively, he must capture and objectify his thoughts, however informally, as written goals and written plans.

DISCUSSION

The Life Planning Model provides a firm foundation for exploring human potential. Its concepts are simple, easy to discuss, and easy to internalize. Many people who are dissatisfied with their lives find the model very appealing. It offers them guidance for thinking about their lives in terms of needs, values, and goals. A person can maintain perspective by frequently reviewing the basic concepts of the model. However, it offers concepts rather than techniques. The question of "How?" requires specific methods and techniques that are part of a group leader's individual capability for helping participants learn about themselves. These techniques constitute an entire subclass of models that can function as companions to the Life Planning Model.

Because of the highly personal nature of the model, it serves best in the informal, low-risk atmosphere of small-group situations where participants can explore its implications. We do not consider the model particularly well-suited to the lecture situation because the one-way communication process does not allow listeners to fully internalize the concepts.

# The Helping Relationship

Gerard Egan designed the Helping Relationship Model to increase the effectiveness and reliability of helping. He describes a repertory of helping skills, structuring the helping process into progressive interdependent stages.

The helping relationship is a special form of temporary interaction between the helper and the helpee, with constructive behavioral change as a primary goal. The helpee is a person who is experiencing difficulty with his life situation and its associated problems because he lacks certain skills of adaptation, coping, and problem solving. The helper is a person who has achieved an acceptable level of personal adjustment, has the skills the helpee lacks, and is able to help the helpee learn those skills.

A departure from traditional approaches to helping, the model places joint responsibility on the helper and helpee. The *helpee*, not the helper, is the principal protagonist in a search for the tools of adjustment. The helpee's task is to come to terms with his life, its problems, and his behavioral patterns, and to develop within himself the necessary skills to manage his life.

A self-defeating symbiotic relationship can result when one person tries to help another with his difficulties. In such a situation, the helpee looks to the helper for the solution to his problems, forming a dependent or manipulative attachment. The helpee may assign general responsibility for his improvement to the helper. The helper, on the other hand, may be tempted into assuming *responsibility and authority* over the helpee. This assumption discounts the helpee's sovereign right and responsibility to manage his own life. Furthermore, it works against the kind of learning the helpee must achieve in order to successfully terminate the helping relationship. To avoid developing a symbiotic relationship at the outset, the helper must possess certain interpersonal skills for managing the course of the transaction.

Attending

A skill of overriding importance, *Attending* refers to the helper's ability to be physically and psychologically "with" the helpee. The helper must be attentive to the helpee's verbal and nonverbal messages and sensitively communicate the fact that he is listening. Attending does *not* require that the helper intervene in any way in the helpee's thought processes. Initially what the helpee needs is acceptance, empathy, and understanding. If the helper yields to the temptation to step in and rescue the helpee from difficulties, he immediately offers to engage in a parent-child relationship that may retard the helpee's progress.

Figure 44 shows the three general phases of the helping relationship, from its inception to its successful—and voluntary—termination. The following defines the nature of the relationship and the activities undertaken by the two participants for each phase.

Clarification

During the first phase of *Clarification*, the helper supports the helpee in his attempts to focus on "what is wrong." In most instances of maladjustment, the beleaguered person is unable to state, in simple, operational terms, what is the matter with him. Once he has achieved this communication, he is usually well on his way toward recovering from his difficulties. During this phase, the helper needs to be available, willing to work on the problem, and able to *respond*. He must *understand* what the helpee is saying, and he must be able to communicate that understanding. This is sometimes referred to as *accurate empathy*, the ability to see the problem from the helpee's frame of reference, undistorted by the helper's own values, opinions, or biases. Respect from the helper is vital; he must demonstrate that he sees the helpee as worthwhile, and that he is *for* him. Finally, the helper must view the clarification phase as the beginning of his facilitation of a *concreteness* that will serve as a firm foundation for the following phases. He must help the person to explore his problem, and to define in language he can easily understand, the thoughts, feelings, and situations that contribute to the problem.

Problem Solving

During the second phase of *Problem Solving*, the helper lends his own experiences to the helpee as a framework for finding solutions. The helper offers models of personal adjustment for the helpee to use in assessing his own coping strategies. The helper brings into play interpersonal skills, such as nondirective listening, clarification, paraphrasing, limited advising, and direct assistance, to assist the helpee in planning feasible courses of action to solve his problem. In this phase, the helper must constantly guard against *inventing*. He can help only to the extent that he is accurate in hearing, interpreting, and organizing. He must not allow his own values or biases to override his perceptions of the problem and of solutions that may work *for the helpee*.

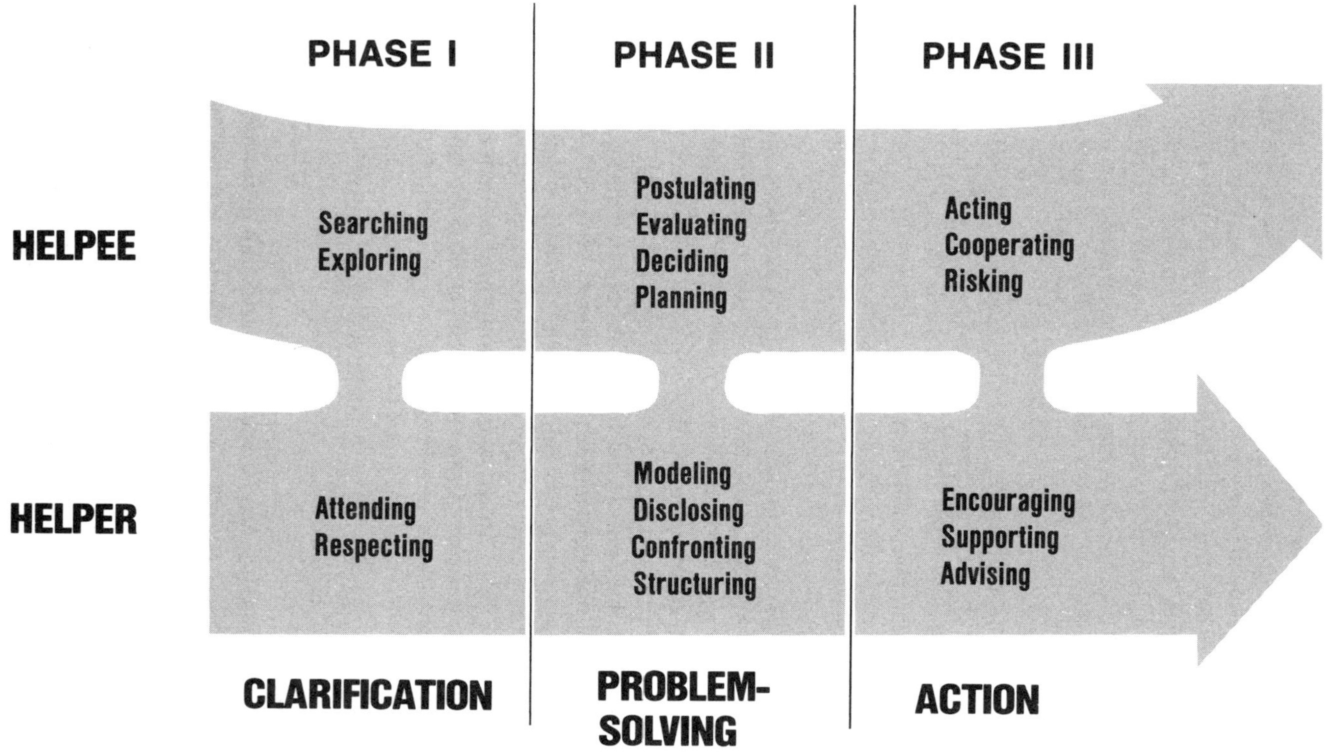

	PHASE I	PHASE II	PHASE III
HELPEE	Searching Exploring	Postulating Evaluating Deciding Planning	Acting Cooperating Risking
HELPER	Attending Respecting	Modeling Disclosing Confronting Structuring	Encouraging Supporting Advising
	CLARIFICATION	**PROBLEM-SOLVING**	**ACTION**

Figure 44. The helping relationship (Adapted from Egan 1975)

As the helper responds to the helpee's disclosures and behavior during this phase, the helpee will need to learn the skills of *non-defensive listening*. Many of the disclosures may be painful and difficult for the helpee to accept. Through the trust and support offered by the helper, the helpee can learn to listen more objectively and completely to the helper's feelings, impressions, and responses. It is not enough for the helpee to understand himself abstractly, he must understand his behavior concretely in terms of its destructive consequences and the need for change.

Action

During the third phase of *Action*, the helper participates with the helpee in making plans and carrying them out. The helpee will need full *attention, respect,* and *support* from the helper if he is to change his behavior toward more constructive and self-fulfilling patterns. The helper should extend himself in any reasonable and human way to help the helpee act on his new plans. The helpee must learn to cooperate, involving himself fully with the helper's efforts to facilitate his new behavior. He must accept the need to take personal risks and to practice risk-taking, increasing the risk in reasonable steps toward his new behavioral objectives. Above all, in this phase, the helpee must begin to *act*. He must practice the skills he is learning, continuing them beyond the helping relationship, to build a fuller and more effective life for himself.

If it will benefit the helpee, the helper should be willing and able to share his own personal experiences and feelings. Through *self-disclosure*, the helper can establish an immediacy with the helpee, exploring the here-and-now of the helping relationship. In that supportive context, the helpee can become more aware of his feelings and behavior. When the helpee experiences difficulty in facing crucial issues, the helper should help him to confront issues in a constructive way. If the helper gives a different perspective to dysfunctional behavior, he can lead the helpee to more accurate and effective ways of viewing himself and his behavior.

DISCUSSION

The Helping Relationship Model bridges a large gap in the study of the helping professions. It suggests for the facilitator, the counselor, the teacher, and others in the helping professions some specific skills and strategies for achieving their goals. Although the model is presented in the context of a dyad relationship, the skills involved are essential to people who are attempting to help in group, classroom, or other more structured situations. The model specifies learning goals for the helper and clearly defines the learning he must facilitate in the helping situation.

People with problems usually feel confused and anxious because of their lack of ability to understand and control the problems confronting them. The helping relationships model can be shared with the helpee so that he can see some organization, structure, and meaning to the helping process. It can give him hope during the early depressing stages and the strength to apply his own resources.

Because a facilitator engages in a series of one-to-one relationships with the people in a group, the model can provide both skills and strategy for enhancing the usefulness of the time they have together.

SUGGESTED READINGS

Brammer, L. *The helping relationship: Process and skills.* Englewood Cliffs, N. J.: Prentice-Hall, 1973.

Carkhuff, R. R. *The art of helping.* Washington, D. C.: American Personnel & Guidance Association, 1972.

Egan, G. *Exercises in helping skills: A training manual to accompany the skilled helper.* Monterey, Calif.: Brooks/Cole, 1975.

Egan, G. *The skilled helper: A model for systematic helping and interpersonal relating.* Monterey, Calif.: Brooks/Cole, 1975.

CONCLUSION TO
PROBLEM-SOLVING MODELS

Experience has not led us to many useful models that are devoted exclusively to the *human processes* of problem-solving. Instead, we have found a large number of problem-solving techniques that are oriented to a very mechanical process, such as the following:

- Gather the facts;
- Organize the data;
- Define the problem;
- List the alternative solutions;
- Select a feasible solution; and
- Implement the solution.

These steps in problem solving represent a category of techniques presented over the years under different names by many people. They completely ignore the drives, emotions, needs, preferences, values, and conflicts that are attendant to most human problems. Furthermore, they are of little use in attacking the type of problem that people frequently refer to as intangible. The techniques may be useful for evaluating alternative business plans or buying a new washing machine, but they offer little help in interpersonal problems.

We have presented models in this section that incorporate some human issues into the problem-solving process. They also are designed for situations the facilitator is likely to encounter.

For the person who can develop problem-solving models that are significant and also easy to understand and apply, there seems to be abundant opportunity.

PART 6
SUPPLEMENTARY CONCEPTS

INTRODUCTION TO
SUPPLEMENTARY CONCEPTS

This part of the book presents a mixed bag of models, almost-models, intriguing concepts, useful analogies, and points of view. They constitute the unclassifiable remainder of our efforts to organize and catalogue models for understanding human behavior. Although we do not consider them appropriate for inclusion as full-fledged models, we find them useful for getting ideas across with impact. Many of them have been in our "bag of tricks" for some time. Others have been discovered during our research for this book.

For these "honorable mention" concepts, we have attempted only to summarize the key ideas. Wherever possible, we offer a reference to some piece of literature that may help the reader to expand on the idea. Where no reference appears, we know of no useful source for further investigation. This is no problem for a number of the concepts because they are so simple that the reader can probably expand on them quite easily.

Many, many other useful almost-models must exist. We make a special plea to our readers to share with us any of the useful little tools and techniques they have found to help people learn about people.

45 Human Bank Account

The term *Human Bank Account* represents the dysfunctional life pattern of connecting one's self-esteem to the opinions, attitudes, and evaluations of others. Typically, someone who behaves like a human bank account feels good when praised, feels hurt and inferior when chided, and feels angry and frustrated when someone offers an insult or a verbal attack. This individual allows others to raise or lower his feelings of self-worth, as though he were powerless to influence those feelings himself.

The analogy to being a bank account—allowing others to make "deposits" and "withdrawals"—offers a convenient label with strong connotations of self-defeating attitudes. A more positive association is the idea of maintaining one's own "balance" of good feelings and self-acceptance.

46 Blind Spots

Humans have a small but distinct blind spot in each eye—images projected on that spot are not perceived. By analogy, each person also has blind spots in his perception of people, ideas, and processes. The individual's brain adapts to his psychological blind spots as it adapts to his optical blind spots. For example, he criticizes certain behavior in others while engaging in it himself; or he excludes certain key factors from his decision process because he has suppressed them below the level of his routine awareness.

The analogy of visual blind spots can be used to introduce group members to the idea of looking for the blind spots in their own personalities. An individual can locate a visual blind spot by closing the left eye, holding his right arm straight forward and focusing his right eye on his right thumbnail. Then he moves his thumb toward the right, but he keeps his eye focused on the spot where his thumb had been. Although he is no longer focusing directly on the moving thumb, it remains in his field of vision until it reaches a point about fifteen degrees from the point of focus. Suddenly, his thumb briefly disappears from his vision—with a striking effect. As his thumb continues moving, it quickly comes into view again. He can explore the size of the blind spot by moving his thumb around in small circles.

After the group reflects on behavioral adaptations to visual blind spots, the leader can extend the discussion to psychological blind spots, eliciting examples from the members.[1] The analogy experience is provocative, intriguing, and easy to remember.

---

1. See Model 17, "The Johari Window."

Relationship Contracts

A Relationship Contract is simply an explicit agreement specifying and ratifying mutual expectations between two people. The value of using the term *contract* is its implication of a strong agreement that both people consider important. Examples might include: a contract between a husband or wife concerning specific matters affecting their children; a contract between a supervisor and an employee about certain aspects of their relationship; or a contract between co-facilitators about their handling of particular situations that could arise in a group situation.

The use of contracts can be extended to many other situations, such as a learning environment, parent/child relationships, client/therapist relationships, or simply relationships between friends. One can even make a contract with himself, as a matter of personal accountability for achievement, growth, or self-actualizing behavior. In some situations, writing down the contract may help to enhance its importance.

Cybernetic vs. Robotlike Thinking

The analogies of robotlike thinking and cybernetic thinking enable participants in creative problem-solving seminars to specify the kind of cognition they wish to strive for and the kind they wish to relinquish.

Much of human thought is habitual, and most people perceive new situations as extended versions of other situations they have experienced. If it constitutes a rigid pattern, habitual thinking can limit an individual's options for dealing with new experiences. The term *robotlike thinking* applies to this overly patterned, mechanistic, stereotyped process of thinking. Other characteristics of robotlike thinking are snap reactions, dogmatic opinions, failure to recognize that others have differing views and values, intolerance of the views or values of others, continually passing judgment on others and their ideas, and assigning people to rigid categories.

On the other hand, *cybernetic thinking* describes the individual who freely deploys his awareness; is alert to new inputs; keeps his opinions, judgments, and attitudes open enough to accept new information, and, above all, is inclined to learn and adapt to new experiences. The term *cybernetic* comes from a Greek form meaning *steersman*, and indeed, the cybernetic thinker is steering his thinking by responding to informational signals and adapting his course to new information.

SUGGESTED READING

Hall, J. T. & Dixon, R. A. Cybernetic sessions: a technique for gathering ideas. In J. W. Pfeiffer & J. E. Jones (Eds.), *The 1974 annual for group facilitators.* La Jolla, Calif.: University Associates, 1974.

Defense Mechanisms in Groups

Growing can be painful. The natural tendency to avoid uncomfortable feelings is demonstrated by a growth group when it levels off and resists further risk of self-exploration. Group members resist further development with defense mechanisms that should be recognized by the facilitator. These defenses have been categorized by Paul Thoresen as follows:

Fight defenses. The individual moves toward a source of conflict with indiscriminate attacking, interrogation, competition with the facilitator, and overall expressions of cynicism.

Flight defenses. The individual moves away from conflict with intellectualization, generalization, projection, attribution, interpretation, and withdrawal.

Group manipulation defenses. The individual chooses more subtle defense mechanisms, including manipulative techniques such as pairing, focusing on one person, and coming to the rescue of someone who is in emotional pain or under social attack.

The facilitator who is aware of these typical defense mechanisms can develop strategies to deal with them.

SUGGESTED READING

Thoresen, P. Defense mechanisms in groups. In J. W. Pfeiffer & J. E. Jones (Eds.), *The 1972 annual handbook for group facilitators.* La Jolla, Calif.: University Associates, 1972.

Emotional Recovery

An individual can adopt a standard strategy for overcoming bad feelings that are dysfunctional for him in a given situation. Such a pattern is advantageous because it can become a habit, easily called upon when necessary. One strategy that works effectively is composed of three questions for a person to ask himself when he becomes aware of being angry, hurt, frustrated, etc.:

What am I feeling?

What am I reacting to?

What am I doing to keep myself feeling this way?

These questions focus the individual's attention on his own responsibility for his feelings, and they introduce a cognitive element into his responses to a situation. This process in itself represents the return to a more functional level of behavior.

SUGGESTED READING

Meininger, J. *Success through transactional analysis.* New York: New American Library, 1974,

51 Ego-Radius

The Ego-Radius Model, designed by Walt Boshear, can be used to evaluate and interrelate items of information an individual knows about himself. The model, diagrammed in Figure 51, represents an individual's ego or *self* (the term is used freely and loosely since few people have a clear idea of what they mean when they say "my*self*") as a circle surrounded by a variety of elements of his existence. The symbol for each element is located according to its postulated psychological distance from the innermost self. For example, if the individual is intensely committed to a profession, then he marks a dot, or some other symbol for profession, quite close to the central symbol for self. If he has little concern for religion, then the symbol for religion is placed farther from the center. To imply relationships between certain factors, they can be clustered within the same area, or perhaps in an angle around the circle. Factors that are in conflict might be placed on opposite sides with the relative distances representing the importance of the conflict.

The model serves as a basic discussion tool for sorting out the processes, people, institutions, and concepts that populate a person's life. Although quite subjective, the process of deciding where to place the symbols can lead individuals into useful considerations of relationships that are important in their lives.

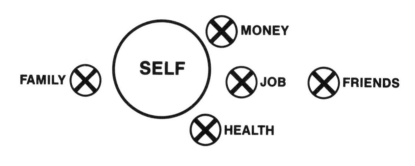

Figure 51. Ego-radius model

Dependency-Intimacy Continuum

Two relatively stable characteristics, *dependency* and *intimacy*, can explain a large part of the variability of a person's reactions to the people with whom he lives and works. Dependency refers to the authority, control, structure, rules, and power demonstrated in relations with other people. Intimacy describes people's characteristic ways of behaving with regard to closeness, personalness, confidentiality, and emotional distance.

If we think of dependency in the usual linear sense, one end of the continuum can stand for *not dependent* and the other end represents *dependent*. Similarly, we might think of intimacy as a matter of degree. We could conclude that the most desirable balance would be a relatively low amount of dependency and a high amount of intimacy. However, according to John E. Jones, it is more useful to think of the dependency continuum and the intimacy continuum as they are displayed graphically in Figure 52.

Extreme feelings of *dependency* can lead to conflicted feelings and dysfunctional behavior. But *counterdependency* may also create problems of rebellion, rejection of authority, and resistance to being influenced by others. Similarly, the opposite extreme from *overintimate* behavior (the need to establish close relationships with everyone) is *counterintimate* behavior (the need to maintain a safe psychological distance from others and to keep relationships formal and impersonal).

Rather than thinking of the optimum values of dependency and intimacy as lying on one end of the scale, it is useful to consider that a more desirable condition is one in which conflicts of dependency and intimacy with other people have been satisfactorily worked out. The middle of each scale, therefore, represents a desirable condition. This model may be used for discussing behavioral options for achieving that middle ground.

SUGGESTED READINGS

Jones, J. E. Dependency-intimacy: A feedback experience. In J. W. Pfeiffer & J. E. Jones (Eds.), *A handbook of structured experiences for human relations training*, Vol. 1. La Jolla, Calif.: University Associates, 1969.

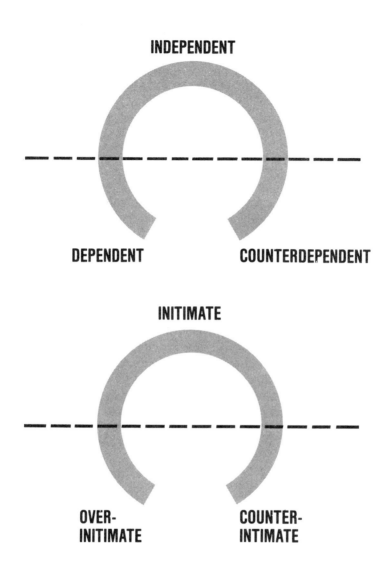

INDEPENDENT

DEPENDENT   COUNTERDEPENDENT

INITIMATE

OVER-   COUNTER-
INITIMATE   INTIMATE

Figure 52. The dependency-intimacy continuum
(Adapted from Jones 1973)

53 Facilitator Functions

A group facilitator's functions are numerous, but Lieberman, Yalom, and Miles identified four that are basic to the facilitator's competency. These are (1) emotional stimulation, (2) caring, (3) meaning attribution, and (4) executive functions. Drawing on numerous sources, Robert Coyne compiled a list of specific behaviors within the four basic functions:

Emotional stimulation includes helping others to contact and release feelings, challenging, confronting, and serving as a catalyst for interaction.

Caring involves accepting, understanding, and supporting others, expressing warmth and affection as a model for others, and helping others to develop intimate relationships.

Meaning attribution calls for giving meaning to experience—helping others to understand and acknowledge the source of their feelings and actions (without simply offering interpretations) and focusing group attention on significant interactions.

Executive functions include reviewing group ground rules, exploring group processes, "gatekeeping," and handling the general logistics of the group meeting.

To be effective, the facilitator must maintain awareness of all four functions and attend to them during his group activities.

SUGGESTED READINGS

Conyne, R. K. Training components for group facilitators. In J. E. Jones & J. W. Pfeiffer (Eds.), *The 1975 annual handbook for group facilitators.* La Jolla, Calif.: University Associates, 1975.

Lieberman, M., Yalom, I., & Miles, M. *Encounter groups: First facts.* New York: Basic Books, 1973.

 **Guidelines for Feedback**

When an individual lets others know his perceptions and feelings about their behavior, he is *giving feedback*. Most participants in growth groups acknowledge the value of feedback for improving interpersonal processes and advancing group progress, but many have had little experience in giving feedback. Their daily experiences take place in contexts that discourage or severely penalize openness and leveling.

One of a facilitator's key functions is to model the process of giving effective feedback. Philip Hanson (1975) specified characteristics of feedback that are productive and those that are counterproductive, such as:

direct rather than indirect expression of feelings;

descriptive rather than attributive or interpretive;

accepting rather than evaluative;

specific rather than general;

respecting an individual's freedom to choose not to change, rather than pressuring him to change;

immediate rather than delayed; and

focused on events shared by the group rather than on external events.

A facilitator can use this checklist to guide group members in giving helpful feedback to one another.

SUGGESTED READING

Hanson, P. G. Giving feedback: An interpersonal skill. In J. E. Jones & J. W. Pfeiffer (Eds.), *The 1975 annual handbook for group facilitators.* La Jolla, Calif.: University Associates, 1975.

55 Hidden Agendas

Just as a group has an agenda for its activities, so each member has a private agenda for his participation. He comes to the group situation with personal needs, goals, expectations, and strategies; left undisclosed and unsatisfied, these become a *hidden agenda*.

Sometimes the hidden agendas of individual members conflict with the group's agenda, leading to behavior that interferes with group processes. By recognizing counterproductive behaviors, the group leader often can detect hidden agendas and deal with them. A useful technique is asking each member to express his desires and expectations for the group's activity or, if there is a group issue, to describe what he considers to be an effective solution.

When hidden agendas are discussed, some may prove to be legitimate concerns that are shared by others. These can be incorporated into the group's general agenda. (Some others are best left under the surface.) The group leader should look for hidden agendas and encourage the group to give some attention to them and evaluate its progress in handling them.

SUGGESTED READING

Hidden agendas. In J. W. Pfeiffer & J. E. Jones (Eds.), *The 1974 annual handbook for group facilitators*. La Jolla, Calif.: University Associates, 1974.

56 Metaverbal Communication

People communicate on more than one level. The most straightforward level is *denotative*—communicating messages verbally. Another, less direct level is *metacommunicative*—communicating about a communication.

Metaverbal messages are communicated by the use of vocal pitch, tone, and juncture, and by using particular words, sentence structures, and strategic omissions of words to convey subtle nuances of meaning "between the lines." A person's internal status—his attitudes, feelings and intentions—may be interpreted from the metaverbal components of his communication.

Many metaverbal messages are inadvertently transmitted. For example, the speaker who begins with "To tell you the truth, . . ." implies that he might not be telling you the truth on other occasions. Another common expression ". . . , you know?" suggests that the speaker feels a slight sense of anxiety about whether the listener accepts or agrees with what he is saying.

Metaverbal forms constitute an interesting and often overlooked area of human communication. By recognizing "meta-talk" and "body language," as well as verbal communication, people can more effectively interpret each other's meaning. This knowledge contributes to a more comprehensive understanding of the ways in which people struggle with their feelings and anxieties while they are trying to make themselves understood.

SUGGESTED READINGS

Nierenberg, G. I. *Meta-talk.* New York: Simon & Schuster, 1973.

Rossiter, C. M., Jr. Making requests through metacommunication. In J. W. Pfeiffer & J. E. Jones (Eds.), *The 1974 annual handbook for group facilitators.* La Jolla, Calif.: University Associates, 1974.

57 Interaction Styles

H. B. Karp suggests that an individual's personality can be viewed as some combination of three functional modes—Tough Battler, Friendly Helper, and Logical Thinker. These are usually represented as the corners of a triangle, as shown in Figure 57.

The triangle can be drawn on newsprint as a discussion tool to help members of a growth group assess their own interaction styles. The participants draw and label the triangle and each marks an X within the triangle to represent his own combination of the three behavioral options. The model can stimulate discussion about combinations of styles, flexibility of one's own style, and ways to deal with individuals who adopt extreme styles.

SUGGESTED READING

Karp, H. B. Re-owning: Increasing behavioral alternatives. In J. W. Pfeiffer & J. E. Jones (Eds.), *The 1974 annual handbook for group facilitators*. La Jolla, Calif.: University Associates, 1974.

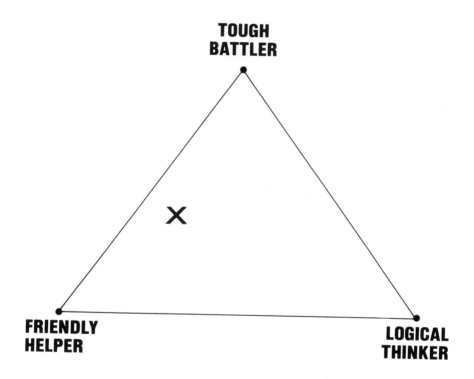

Figure 57. Interaction styles

58 Imaginary Interactors

When two people are interacting with each other on a specific occasion, it could be said that four personalities are actually represented. Two of the personalities are imaginary, but they play an extremely important part in the interaction—which amounts to the *Real You* sending messages to the *Imaginary Him*, and the *Real Him* sending messages to the *Imaginary You*. The Imaginary Him is the person you *believe* him to be. Because you never can occupy the other person's life space or duplicate his past experiences, you never will know what it is like to *be* him. You can surmise what he is like only by making inferences from his external behavior. Similarly, he can make inferences about you only from your behavior.

To the extent that the imaginary images coincide with the real persons, effective communication can take place. The communication area where the imaginary and real personalities overlap can be represented by two intersecting circles for each person, with vectors drawn between the circles to indicate interpersonal messages, as shown in Figure 58.

This model is useful in discussions of two-person communication and interpersonal relationships.

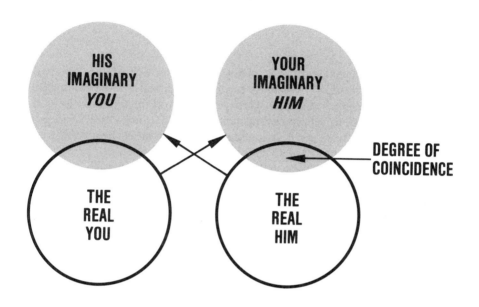

Figure 58. Imaginary interactors

Risk-Taking Styles

An individual's decision-making behavior in a situation of uncertainty or risk can be considered a strategy for protecting himself against making the wrong choice. This individual error-protection style tends to be consistent and well-defined. In making a risk decision, one faces two kinds of inferential errors that John E. Jones identified (with labels borrowed from statistical analysis) as Type I and Type II errors.

A Type I error is a *false positive* decision: a prediction is made that a certain outcome *will* occur, but it *does not*. The inverse of this, a Type II error, is a *false negative* decision: a prediction is made that a certain thing *will not* happen, but it *does*. These two kinds of errors are reciprocally related; insuring against one of them increases the probability of making the other. For example, Arnold may want to strike up a conversation with a woman in a restaurant. If he wants to avoid the possible embarrassment of rejection, he may reveal his reluctance by approaching the woman timidly or passing up the opportunity. In this case, Arnold is protecting himself from a Type I error. That is, he wants to avoid the problem of expecting a positive outcome and experiencing a negative one. On the other hand, Arnold may want to avoid the risk of missing an enjoyable experience he might have if the woman responds in a friendly way. If he takes the risk and approaches the woman, he is protecting himself from a Type II error.

The major decision-making styles of people can be classified according to whether they protect themselves against Type I errors ("sins of commission") or Type II errors ("sins of omission"). Type I protectors tend to approach the world with caution; they are low risk-takers. Conversely, Type II protectors test themselves against the world, reaching out for its possibilities and taking their chances.

SUGGESTED READING

Jones, J. E. Risk-taking and error protection styles. In J. W. Pfeiffer & J. E. Jones (Eds.), *The 1972 annual handbook for group facilitators*. La Jolla, Calif.: University Associates, 1972.

60 Santa Claus Fantasy

Santa Claus Fantasy is a deprecating metaphor for a pattern of behavior characterized by an individual's passivity, lack of self-direction, dependency, desire for security, unwillingness to make basic life decisions, and general exasperation with life. Such an individual seems to be waiting for some external power figure—Santa Claus or the Good Fairy or the Knight on a White Horse—to come along and release him from a life of unhappiness. His conversation and actions imply that the responsibility for his success and happiness is to be found somewhere in the external world, rather than in his own attitudes. Eric Berne referred to this syndrome as "waiting in Destiny's bus station" for a bus (that will never come) to take one to happiness.

The alternatives to the Santa Claus Fantasy are self-acceptance, assumption of the executive function in one's own life, and goal-directed activity.

SUGGESTED READING

Berne, E. *What do you say after you say hello?* New York: Bantam Books, 1973.

 **Thinking Tools**

There are six useful verbal tools that amount to semantic antidotes to rigid thinking and communication. The following semantic tools can help to focus an individual's attention on the complexity of human processes and to remind him of the dangers of overgeneralizing and categorizing:

- *"So far as I know"* expresses the speaker's recognition that other important information lies beyond the range of one's awareness;
- *"Up to a point"* indicates avoidance of extremes and either/or thinking and communication;
- *"To me"* demonstrates recognition of one's subjective knowledge and biases and acceptance of someone else's sovereignty, knowledge, and value system;
- Differentiating one man from the class of all men shows that the speaker is dealing with a person as an individual rather than as a member of a stereotyped class;
- Recognizing one's environment as a *process* rather than a static place acknowledges that the world and people in it change continuously; and
- Recognizing that a situation plays an important part in the processes one is trying to describe indicates the speaker's sense of context; for example, a teenager among his peers behaves differently than he does at home, in school, or in church.

SUGGESTED READING

Keyes, K., Jr. *How to develop your thinking ability.* New York: McGraw-Hill, 1950.

62 Self-Made Traps

Self-Made Traps are the undesirable results of rigidly patterned, programmed forms of behavior that an individual fails to evaluate. Examples are the role trap, the ego trap, and the activity trap.

In the *role trap*, an individual feels he must assume and defend a specified role toward others, such as The Boss, The Expert, The Teacher, The Parent, and The Sophisticate. There are many of these rigid roles. An individual's acceptance of one of them blocks off many behavioral options because he feels compelled to maintain the role when more flexible behavior would achieve more desirable results.

A person falls into the *ego trap* when he identifies his integrity or self-esteem with some enterprise to which he assigns value. This identification results in dysfunctional adaptations, such as the salesman's feeling of rejection when his prospect decides not to buy his product. He cannot differentiate between rejection of the product and rejection of himself as a person.

The *activity trap* results from confusing activity with results. When groups lack clearly specified objectives, the members often resort to activity for its own sake. This provides a means for structuring their time, which reduces anxiety about interpersonal processes.

 **Types of Problems**

Three general types of problems can be identified for the purpose of studying creative problem solving. Although two of these problems are easily recognizable, the third is often overlooked.

Insufficient information. An individual may recognize and clearly state a problem, but he may lack the required information to solve it. In such a case, he will strive to reduce his uncertainty.

Inadequate structure. A person has sufficient information, but he does not know how to arrange it to achieve an effective solution. This situation calls for new, novel, or unorthodox concepts to lend structure to the information.

No problem. The adequacy of the available solution blocks perception of the situation as a problem. For example, a business organization may have an orthodox relationship with its employees through their labor union. As long as this relationship is perceived as the only way to do business, "there is no problem." But a prolonged labor strike may cause the company to examine basic assumptions and constraints. It then becomes possible to identify a *situation that needs attention.* Looking beyond the no-problem state of affairs (in this case, *before* the strike) requires a particular mental approach, which can be developed and encouraged by training in creative problem solving.

SUGGESTED READING

De Bono, E. *Lateral thinking: Creativity step by step.* New York: Harper & Row, 1970.

 **Human Vending Machine**

The metaphor Human Vending Machine helps to focus attention on the self-defeating habit of *signal reactions*—an immediate, unthinking response to a provocation. The response has been called by other names, including snap reaction, knee-jerk reaction, rectal response, spinal thinking, and mechanical judgment. All of these terms imply the seemingly involuntary condition of an individual who automatically "vends" a programmed response whenever someone provides the proper "coin." For example, a simple teasing remark may produce immediate anger, frustration, or hurt feelings in the recipient.

A person can counteract this dysfunctional pattern by accepting responsibility for his own feelings and responses and modifying his reactions to the behavior of others in accordance with a high level of self-acceptance and self-esteem.

SUGGESTED READING

Johnson, W. *People in quandaries.* New York: Harper & Row, 1946.

PART 7

APPLICATION OF MODELS

APPLICATION OF
MODELS

Readers who are conversant with system sciences will recognize a central theme throughout this book. That theme is behavioral synthesis—the organizing of selected aspects of behavior into a unified structure. The structure itself becomes valuable in helping to understand the relationships among the concepts. This is fundamentally a systems engineering approach to a subject that traditionally has been considered too complex to be analyzed.

Those who have advanced the most important ideas in the behavioral science field have, in fact, created systematic models and these have proven their value. Although speculation, conjecture, and especially labeling and classifying constitutes the bulk of behavioral science work, the significant contributions to the *communication* of these ideas has been the development of simple conceptual models.

We believe we are embarked on a major new thrust in the behavioral sciences—the development of *human systems engineering*. Development in this area is in a primitive stage, and it is much in need of creative contributions from the many human relations practitioners.

Planning with and Around Models

Models may be used in a number of ways as planning tools for learning experiences. The experience itself may be modeled as a way of anticipating the demands upon the facilitator.

One technique we frequently use for planning a semistructured session was developed by Walt Boshear. As shown in Figure B, the horizontal axis in the diagram represents the time available with the participants, in this case, one twelve-hour day. The vertical axis can represent any other variable relevant to the facilitator. In the following example, the

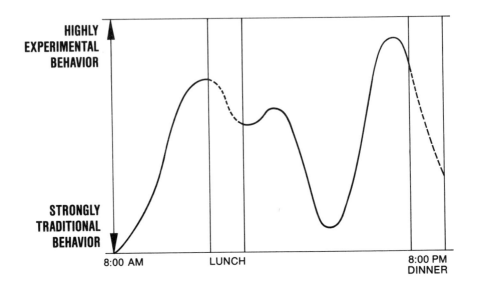

Figure B. Planning a semi-structured learning experience

vertical axis represents (subjectively, of course) the relative degree of experimental behavior we hope to lead the group to experience.

> The participants enter the room at 8:00 A.M. in their traditional roles. By noon, we facilitate a moderately high degree of experimental behavior. During lunch, the participants are expected to "drift" back toward the more patterned behavior. After lunch, we return briefly to a more experimental mode, then facilitate a quick return to fairly safe traditional modes of behavior to review the experiences of the day. We want to demonstrate that the group experience was not accidental, and that the participants can return to the experimental mode any time they desire. To accomplish this, we facilitate a brief, but intense, encounter between the participants before winding up the day with a traditional closure activity.

We may prepare and discuss several plans for one session, each represented by its own model. The graphic representation of our ideas helps us to communicate about our hopes and expectations for the experience, and to discuss techniques and alternative strategies. During the session, the retained image of the graph allows us to evaluate and quickly communicate the degree to which we are proceeding according to plan.

Once we agree upon a plan, we can discuss the "tools" we may need to implement our plan and the role each of us will have in the process, according to our respective strengths and weaknesses.

This planning technique leads naturally to a discussion of which structured experiences may be most effective at each step along the way and which models may be useful. In this way, we can anticipate, generally, the need for a model to facilitate a process and can "bone-up" on that model, and, if necessary, prepare handouts.

Using Models in Group Situations

A learning situation might call for theoretical input to enable the participants to explore new possibilities for thinking about behavior. For this purpose, certain basic models simplify the learning process, shorten presentation time, and help participants to retain primary concepts. Because each model (as we define it) includes some diagrammatic representation of behavioral processes, it provides a channel for quick and efficient explanation. Once a diagram or a sketch is before the group, on a chalkboard or a newsprint pad, anyone can point to it or modify it while discussing the basic ideas it incorporates. This "tangible" aspect of behavioral models is influential in the learning process.

In the seminar/workshop environment, models provide practical experience with the key concepts of behavior. For example, having introduced the Ego States: Parent/Adult/Child Model from transactional analysis, the facilitator can proceed to deal with any one of the ego states.

In helping participants to identify and recognize the Child state, we frequently use fantasy experiences or re-enactment of childhood feelings. In such a case, the model provides a guiding framework for the learning process. As a structured way of looking at unfamiliar processes, the model tends to create an attitude of acceptance; it makes sense to the participant. Models are especially helpful in dealing with sophisticated, rigidly "programmed" individuals, such as some business managers and some professionals. Many of these people seem to adopt a defensive, evasive attitude toward feelings and close interpersonal processes. The model enables the facilitator to account for the participant's current coping strategies, and to "start where he is."

As an adjunct to more common encounter techniques, we make extensive use of semistructured processes. These often consist of a combination of cognitive inputs, supported by behavioral models, and direct personal experience through facilitator-guided activities. Although these learning modules do not substitute for the intensity of the unstructured direct encounter, they often serve to accelerate a group's progress.

We do not believe in fully unstructured situations for their own sake, but rather as strategically selected options for a total learning process. Participants need to "buy into" the group experience, not merely as a matter of risk-taking or gambling on their own growth, but as a conscious decision based on a reasonable expectation that they will have opportunities to learn. The semistructured approach is an effective foundation for this phase of the learning experience.

An Inventory of Models

The group leader or facilitator who has at his disposal a number of different models for understanding behavior can help a group to approach the subject from a variety of directions. There are many practitioners of special theories of psychology who have made important contributions to the field. However, the line between interest and obsession—where one's own theory is concerned—is exceedingly thin. Having a large inventory of models helps the facilitator to avoid becoming imprisoned by any one framework in dealing with specific human processes.

Each model has a *limited* domain of applicability. Within those boundaries, and subject to its own structural limitations, the model serves a useful function. But, extended beyond its proper limits, it can become treacherous, suggesting things about human behavior that simply are not represented in the real world. *Before* this becomes a problem, the model should be exchanged for one more nearly suited to the situation at hand—if one exists. The more tools the group leader has at his disposal, the less likely he is to use them inappropriately. As Maslow observed, "When the only tool you have is a hammer, you tend to treat everything as if it were a nail."

Pitfalls in Using Models

We have seen (and have been guilty of) several kinds of misapplication of behavioral models. The typical pitfalls in using models fall into three broad categories:

1. Trying to stretch the model to cover too many situations, variations, or features of behavior;
2. Uncritically accepting false inferences indicated by the model; and,
3. Becoming deluded by "geometrical" features that portray aspects of behavior which are not true to life.

The first pitfall, unwillingness to trade the model for another, is perhaps the most common. With a framework as broad and comprehensive as the Parent/Adult/Child ego-state model, one may be tempted to try to extend it further and further. This may result in a patchwork of new terms, distortions of the basic concepts, and forced explanations of behavior in the jargon of transactional analysis. This is not to say that the TA model is wrong, but that another model may be more appropriate to the situation at hand. For example, in dealing with decision-making processes, one could use the Adult and Parent states to discuss cognitive processes. But a much more useful vehicle might be Festinger's Cognitive Dissonance Model, or deBono's Lateral Thinking Model. Similarly, Maslow's Hierarchy of Needs Model is useful in discussing motivation and goal-directed behavior, but one might find TA more useful in dealing with personal values and attitudes. Deciding which model to use—and when to abandon it—should be a constant concern of the facilitator.

The second pitfall, accepting false inferences, is a more subtle one. An example of this may be found in the OK/NOT-OK Life Positions Model, which represents a person as embracing one of four possible assumptions about himself and his relationships with others. There are: (1) I'm NOT-OK, You're OK; (2) I'm NOT-OK, You're NOT-OK; (3) I'm OK, You're NOT-OK; and (4) I'm OK, You're OK. Position number three, I'm OK, You're NOT-OK, is a highly maladjusted orientation. It is often the position adopted by the battered child or the psychotic adult. However, the terminology of the model implies that the OK of this position is the same as the OK of the fourth position—the self-actualizing one—I'm OK, You're OK. This is completely false. The third-position OK, founded in hatred, resentment, and distorted thinking, is not the same healthy, life-supporting assumption as the fourth-position OK.

To make matters more confusing, the accompanying diagram, sometimes whimsically labeled the OK Corral, portrays the four life positions as corners of a continuous plane. The implication that one can move around within this field of relative OK-ness is very misleading. The transition from NOT-OK to OK, or from the negative I'm OK to the positive I'm OK is an intellectual leap. The individual must recognize and acknowledge the self-defeating character of his life position, and *decide* to abandon it for a more healthy one. The model does not clearly account for this concept. This does not, of course, invalidate the model, but it raises a serious warning for those who would conclude that any inference drawn from the model is represented in life.

The third pitfall in using models, misleading geometry, frequently goes unrecognized, yet it sometimes exerts a strong influence on the thought processes of those who use certain models. For example, the Maslow Hierarchy of Needs Model is customarily represented by a triangle or a pyramid of needs. Most users of the model label the top of the pyramid *Self-Actualization*, and the bottom *Basic Needs*. Because of our cultural biases toward geometric symbology, the top of the needs hierarchy appears to represent needs that are somehow better or more positive than those at the bottom. This results in an unconscious infusion of values into the model.

All of these pitfalls stem from one basic mistake in constructing and using models: failure to recognize that any model is an abstraction—an analogy created to help one think about the underlying process. As such, it is inevitably limited to some narrow range of appropriate functions. This is fundamental because *the model is not the process*. The primary advantage of any useful behavioral model is, in fact, its limited scope. It deals with selected features of human behavior within a context that is bounded to permit convenient study. This characteristic of a model is simultaneously an asset and a liability.

Creating Models—How and Why

Constructing models is not a magical process. It requires no particular technical training. Rather, it involves a basic *point of view*—an impulse to synthesize, to organize, to interrelate what we know about human beings. We have constructed several of the models in this book ourselves, out of a need to understand certain features of behavior. One of the models was inadvertently created out of a need to come to terms with a personal emotional shock. The conceptual framework arose from the process of thinking through the disturbance and seeking strategies for dealing with it. Other practitioners have constructed models under the same circumstances, and similarly, the reader can contribute models to the behavioral sciences field.

To stimulate model building, we offer a problem that includes all of the basic features of a situation in need of a model. To avoid the possibility of theoretical or philosophical pitfalls, this is a simple physical problem rather than a behavioral one. It should be obvious that studying an intrapersonal or interpersonal *process* would involve more complexity than this problem, but the model-building process would be much the same. The problem has only one answer. We are concerned here only with *functions*, not with the *content* of the model. As the reader follows the development of the model, he should pay close attention to the thought process involved in organizing the information.

Consider the following situation:

Three ordinary playing cards are lying face down on a table. The following information (for some reason) is known about the cards.

1. To the left of a Queen there is a Jack.
2. To the left of a Spade there is a Diamond.
3. To the right of a Heart there is a King.
4. To the right of a King there is a Spade.

Solve the following problem:

Identify the proper suit for each face card.

This situation is analogous to many life situations, in that it presents a body of disconnected information. Some simplifying relationships could aid toward understanding the situation. One's first impulse might be to try to randomly associate the suits with the cards. A second possibility would be to write all possible combinations of the three cards and three suits, and then test each arrangement until the correct one is found. A third possibility, which represents a creative jump, is to devise some kind of abstract *system* or method—organizing the known information in a manner that leads to the unknown information. This, indeed, is a model.

Figure C shows one possibility for modeling this problem. The model in this case, consists of:

- The four elements of known *information*, in addition to the general picture of the situation (playing cards, suits, etc.)
- The *structure* provided by a matrix diagram
- The *relationships* that are clarified by the structure

	LEFT	MIDDLE	RIGHT
LEFT	MIDDLE	RIGHT	

	LEFT	MIDDLE	RIGHT
(King)			
(Queen)	1. IMPOSSIBLE		
(Jack)			1. IMPOSSIBLE
♠	2. IMPOSSIBLE		
♥			
♦			2. IMPOSSIBLE

1. "To the left of a Queen there is a Jack."
2. "To the left of a Spade there is a Diamond."
3. ...
4. ...etc.

Figure C. Construction of a matrix model for an artificial problem selected for demonstration purposes (first two steps)

These three features—information, structure, and relationships—are the basic defining characteristics of the model. The following are the dynamics of the model, i.e., how to use it to derive new information:

> Advance by a process of elimination, putting an X in each square of the matrix that represents an impossible combination of face card and suit. For example, the statement, "To the left of a Queen there is a Jack," implies that the Queen cannot be the card to the far left because then the Jack could not be to her left. Conversely, the Jack cannot be the card to the far right because the Queen must be to his right. To confirm this reasoning process, analyze the second statement, "To the left of a Spade there is a Diamond." This implies that the Spade cannot be the card to the far left. It also means that the Diamond cannot be the card to the far right. Continue in this manner, eliminating impossible combinations and recording them in the matrix until left with only one possible face card and only one possible suit for each position.

A review of the functions of the model reveals that, first, it offers a way to *visualize* the situation. It gives an image of three cards—left, middle, and right—and provides a pigeonhole for each of the six possibilities for each position—three faces and three suits. Secondly, inferences can be made *about the underlying situation being modeled*, which are not obvious from the given information. The structure of the model serves to clarify hidden relationships. An important part of the modeling process is the checking of inferences against the real world, which, in this case, requires arranging the cards on a table to see if the correct solution has been reached.

The very same functions used with the example are performed by behavioral models. Of course, the underlying processes are immeasurably more complex, but this is a matter of application rather than of concept. At this point, it might be helpful to review the working definition of a model, given in the introduction to this book. While reflecting on the models presented in the various sections, the reader should recognize their common features.

Modeling Techniques

The model constructed for the example exploys a matrix diagram to arrange the key elements of information. Matrix diagrams represent a large class of modeling techniques, but they are by no means the only important ones. Others include linear scales (continuous variables), co-ordinate systems (or spatial models), cartoons, diagrams, and graphs. These are not models, but are the tools of the model-maker's art. It is only when they are well married to key elements of information, that these tools take on the useful character of behavioral models.

The selection of a technique for a particular application is an important part of the modeling process. Selecting a "two-state" method of illustrating a linear process can lead the model builder into many traps. The model builder must be bold enough to make a tentative selection of a technique, but courageous enough to throw it out if it begins to break down. Sometimes, it may take two or three diagrams to present an idea simply and clearly. Attempting to incorporate the entire idea into one diagram may result in a complexity that defeats the original purpose—communication.

We must frequently remind ourselves of why we are modeling human characteristics and human behavior. The principal reason is to communicate—with oneself by organizing and clarifying our own ideas, and with others by transferring those ideas to them. This caution helps us to avoid becoming enamored of models for their own sakes. Several models we reviewed during the preparation of this book were conceptually sound and well developed, but they were virtually useless for communicating. They were so complex and intricate that the essence of a model was almost impossible to perceive.

Where Do We Go From Here?

This book is a beginning at organizing much of what has been done so far in the development of useful behavioral models. Many other models that escaped us are probably as valuable as the ones we selected. To recapitulate, these models were selected because: (1) they illuminate basic human processes; (2) they are simple, portable, and easy to deal with; and (3) they are useful in helping people to learn about people.

It is our hope that many readers of this book will develop enough interest in the emerging discipline of human systems engineering to pursue it. We would like to hear of their efforts, their ideas, and—most of all—their favorite models.

INDEX